COMPANION TRAVEL GUIDE TO

ČESKÝ KRUMLOV, CZECH REPUBLIC

Must See, Must Do Activities! Top Attractions! insider and Local Tips! Cultural Immersion!

CARL DIAZ

COPYRIGHT NOTICE

This publication is copyright-protected. This is only for personal use. No part of this publication may be, reproduced, in any form or medium, stored in a data retrieval system or transmitted by or through any means, without prior written permission from the Author.

Legal action will be pursued if this is breached.

SCAN HERE TO GAIN ACCESS TO ALL MY BOOKS

DISCLAIMER

Please note that the information contained within this document is for educational purposes only. The information contained herein has been obtained from sources believed to be reliable at the time of publication. The opinions expressed herein are subject to change without notice. Readers acknowledge that the Author / Publisher is not engaging in rendering legal, financial or professional advice.

The Publisher / Author disclaims all warranties as to the accuracy, completeness, or adequacy of such information.

The Publisher assumes no liability for errors, omissions, or inadequacies in the information contained herein or from the interpretations thereof. The publisher / Author specifically disclaims any liability from the use or application of the information contained herein or from the interpretations thereof.

Contents

DISCLAIMER 3
INTRODUCTION 9
   About Český Krumlov. 9
   Why visit Český Krumlov? 12
   How To Use This Guide: 14
Chapter 1 16
PLANNING YOUR TRIP 16
   When to visit Český Krumlov? 16
      Summer (June to August) 16
      Spring (April to May) and Autumn (September to October) 18
      Winter (December - February). 20
   Duration of Stay Recommendations 22
   Weather and Climate Information 25
      Additional weather tips: 27
   How to Get There 28
      By Air 28
      By Train 32
      By Bus 39
      By Car 42
   Visa and Entry Requirements 46
Chapter 2 49
TOP TOURIST ATTRACTIONS 49

Český Krumlov Castle... 49

Historic City Center 53

Egon Schiele Art Centrum... 56

Český Krumlov Regional Museum 58

St. Vitus Church 62

Český Krumlov Baroque Theater 64

Vltava River Rafting and Canoeing 68

Brewery Tours... 72

Bear Sanctuary... 76

Chapter 3.. 81

WHAT TO DO AND NOT TO DO... 81

Cultural Etiquette 81

Respectful behavior toward locals. 82

Safety Tips... 84

Environmental Responsibility 86

Chapter 4.. 89

ACCOMMODATION OPTIONS 89

Hotels 89

Guesthouses and Bed & Breakfasts 91

Apartments and Vacation Rentals 92

Top Recommended Hotels and Resorts 94

Choosing the Right Accommodation for You. 96

Booking Tips and Tricks 97

Booking Platforms 98

Chapter 5 101

TRANSPORTATION WITHIN ČESKÝ KRUMLOV 101

Chapter 6 105

DINING AND CULINARY EXPERIENCES 105

   Traditional Czech cuisine: 105

      Where to Find Traditional Czech Cuisine in Český Krumlov? 108

   Local Specialties: 109

   Fine Dining Restaurants and Cafés in Český Krumlov 111

      Tips for Dining in Český Krumlov. 115

Chapter 7 117

SHOPPING AND ENTERTAINMENT IN ČESKÝ KRUMLOV. 117

   Shopping 117

      Local souvenirs and handicrafts: 117

      Art Galleries and Studios: 120

      Fashion and Jewelry Boutiques: 123

   Entertainment: 126

      Cultural Performances: 126

      Live Music and Nightlife: 130

      Outdoor Activities and Events: 133

Chapter 8 137

ITINERARIES FOR DIFFERENT TRAVELERS 137

   Weekend Getaway 137

      Day 1 137

- Day 2 138
- Cultural Immersion 139
  - Day 1 139
  - Day 2 140
- Adventure Seekers Itinerary 141
  - Day 1 141
  - Day 2 142
- Family-Friendly Itinerary 143
  - Day 1 143
  - Day 2 144
- Budget Travel 145
  - Day 1 145
  - Day 2 146
- Romantic Getaway Itinerary 147
  - Day 1 147
  - Day 2 148

Chapter 9 150
EVENTS AND FESTIVALS 150
Chapter 10 155
PRACTICAL TIPS 155
- Packing essentials: 155
- Currency and payment: 156
- Language and Communication: 160
- WiFi and Connectivity: 164

    Sustainable Travel Practices: 167
    Health & Wellness: 167
CONCLUSION 169
    Final Tips and Recommendations 169
APPENDIX: USEFUL RESOURCES 171
    Emergency Contacts 171
    Maps and Navigational Tools 172
    Additional Reading and References 173
    Useful Local Phrases 174

INTRODUCTION

Welcome to Český Krumlov, a charming and attractive village in the Czech Republic. I'm delighted to accompany you on your excursion through cobblestone streets, ancient architecture, and the rich history of this UNESCO World Heritage Site.

About Český Krumlov.

A town that feels like a living, breathing storybook come to life. Let me take you on a deeper dive into what makes this South Bohemia treasure so wonderful.

A Living Heritage

The noble House of Krumlov created Český Krumlov over 700 years ago, beginning its history. From its humble origins as a small village, the town flourished into a thriving hub of trade and culture, attracting artisans, merchants, and lords from all over.

One of the town's most notable features is its magnificent castle, which dominates the skyline and serves as a reminder of its storied past. Originally constructed in the 13th century, the castle has seen multiple additions and modifications over the ages, culminating in a spectacular complex that combines Gothic, Renaissance, and Baroque architectural styles.

A UNESCO World Heritage Site.

In 1992, Český Krumlov was added to the UNESCO World Heritage List, highlighting its cultural significance and well-preserved architecture. As you walk through the maze of narrow streets and alleyways, you'll come across a plethora of historical treasures, including centuries-old churches and chapels, elegant fountains, and hidden courtyards.

A Cultural Melting Pot

Český Krumlov has been influenced by many different cultures, including Czech, German, Jewish, and Italian. This cultural melting pot is mirrored in the town's architecture, cuisine, and traditions, resulting in a rich tapestry of heritage just waiting to be discovered.

A Town of Festivals and Events

Immerse yourself in Český Krumlov's bustling calendar of festivals and events to truly experience the city's character. There's always something going on in Český Krumlov, from the annual Five-Petalled Rose Festival to the International Music Festival, which showcases world-class performances in stunning historical venues.

A Gateway to Nature.

Český Krumlov offers both intriguing architecture and cultural attractions, as well as access to South Bohemia's natural splendor. Just a short drive or hike away, you'll be surrounded by rolling hills, lush forests, and quiet rivers, ideal for outdoor activities like as hiking, cycling, fishing, and kayaking.

A warm welcome awaits.

The residents of Český Krumlov are known for their friendliness and hospitality, which is possibly its greatest lasting appeal. Whether you're conversing with locals in a comfortable pub, buying handmade items at a market stall, or dining on traditional Czech cuisine at a family-owned restaurant, you'll be greeted with real warmth and kindness at every step.

Why visit Český Krumlov?

Immersive History and Architecture.

The rich history and architectural marvels of Český Krumlov make it a must-see destination. As you walk through the meandering lanes of the old city center, you'll be taken back to the medieval age. The town's crown treasure, Český Krumlov Castle, is a masterpiece of Gothic, Renaissance, and Baroque architecture, affording a look into centuries of aristocratic life. Inside the castle complex, you may explore rich interiors such as the Castle Museum, the Castle Tower with panoramic views, and the stunning Castle Gardens, which are filled with statues and fountains.

Beyond the castle, the entire town is a UNESCO World Heritage Site, with an impressive collection of well-preserved buildings and sites. Český Krumlov's rich history is evident in every corner, from the finely decorated interior of St. Vitus Church to the attractive Renaissance and Baroque residences bordering the streets.

Vibrant Cultural Scene

Český Krumlov is not only historically significant, but also a cultural hub where visitors may immerse themselves in the region's arts and traditions. Throughout the year, the town organizes a number of festivals, concerts, and theatrical performances, ranging from classical music to contemporary art.

The Český Krumlov Baroque Theater, one of the world's best-preserved, is a must-see for cultural fans. You can see authentic performances of Baroque operas, ballets, and dramas that transport you back to the golden days of the Habsburg Empire.

Scenic Natural Beauty.

Český Krumlov is not only a historical and cultural destination, but also a nature lover's heaven. Surrounded by the undulating hills of South Bohemia and the trickling Vltava River, the town provides several chances for outdoor adventure and discovery.

To fully appreciate the natural splendor of Český Krumlov, take a stroll along the riverbanks or rent a kayak or canoe for a relaxing paddle downstream. The lovely environment offers hiking and cycling options, with routes leading to secret waterfalls, scenic vistas, and attractive villages.

Quaint Charm and Local Flavors

Český Krumlov distinguishes itself by combining old-world beauty with modern amenities. Despite its prominence as a tourist attraction, the town has maintained its original feel, with family-owned businesses, artisan stores, and charming cafes nestled in centuries-old structures.

As you meander around the cobblestone streets, don't forget to sample the local cuisine and flavors. Český Krumlov's gastronomic offerings include traditional Czech dishes like goulash and dumplings, as well as locally brewed beers.

How To Use This Guide:

As you prepare for your trip to Český Krumlov, here's a quick explanation of how to use this guide.

Consider it your personal guide to touring the town and its surroundings.

Each chapter is intended to provide you with all of the information you need to plan your trip, from practical instructions on transportation and lodging to recommendations on top sights, activities, and itineraries. Whether you're a first-time visitor or a returning traveler, Český Krumlov's hidden gems provide something for everyone.

Relax and experience the enchantment of Český Krumlov together. Believe me, you're in for an incredible experience!

Chapter 1

PLANNING YOUR TRIP

If you're planning an adventure in Český Krumlov, you are in for a treat! Let's look at some crucial planning ideas to make your vacation as seamless as possible.

When to visit Český Krumlov?

Summer (June to August)

Summer is the most popular tourist season in Český Krumlov, and for good reason. The weather is warm and pleasant, ideal for visiting the city's outdoor attractions and taking in its colorful atmosphere. During this season, daytime hours will be longer, with the sun sinking as late as 9 or 10 p.m., giving you plenty of time to walk the cobblestone streets and relax by the river.

However, the good weather brings crowds. The streets of Český Krumlov can be congested, especially near major sights like the castle and town center. If you don't mind rubbing shoulders with other travelers and prefer a lively atmosphere, summer is the best season to visit.

Summer offers a variety of cultural events and festivals in Český Krumlov, adding to the thrill of your trip. During the summer, there is usually something going on in the city, from outdoor concerts and theatre performances to traditional folk festivals and craft markets.

Activities that can be done

- **Rafting and Canoeing on the Vltava River:** The summer months are great for water sports on the scenic Vltava River. Rent a canoe or join a guided rafting tour to explore the beautiful region around Český Krumlov. Enjoy breathtaking vistas of rolling hills, thick forests, and medieval castles along the route.

- **Open-Air Festivals and Concerts:** Český Krumlov comes alive with music, art, and culture during the summer months, with a variety of outdoor festivals and concerts taking place throughout the city. Everyone may find something to enjoy, from classical music performances in the castle courtyard to boisterous street festivals celebrating Czech traditions.

- **Al Fresco Dining:** Take advantage of the warm weather by dining al fresco at one of Český Krumlov's charming cafes or riverside restaurants. Enjoy traditional Czech meals and local delights while admiring the city's historic architecture and natural beauty.

Spring (April to May) and Autumn (September to October)

For those who prefer a quieter, more laid-back atmosphere, spring and autumn are excellent times to visit Český Krumlov. During the shoulder seasons, the weather is temperate and pleasant, making it excellent for outdoor activities such as hiking, cycling, and walking around town.

Spring brings the blooming of flowers and trees, which paints the environment with bright hues and fills the air with a refreshing aroma. Spring is a perfect season to experience the beauty of Český Krumlov's parks and gardens, as nature begins to bloom after the winter months.

Autumn, on the other hand, is distinguished by breathtaking foliage as the leaves change color, providing a magnificent backdrop for your activities. The colder temperatures are ideal for long walks along the riverbank or leisurely strolls around the historic district.

During the spring and autumn, there are fewer tourists in the city, allowing you to have a more real and intimate experience. In addition, during these off-peak seasons, lodgings and attractions may offer lower prices and special discounts, making it a more affordable option for travelers.

Activities that can be done

- **Scenic Hiking and Cycling:** Explore Český Krumlov's picturesque paths and pathways by hiking or biking. There are numerous outdoor activities available, ranging from easy strolls along the Vltava River to strenuous excursions up adjacent hills and mountains.

- **Wine Tasting in the Vineyards:** Český Krumlov is surrounded by lush vineyards producing some of the finest wines in the Czech Republic. A wine tasting tour allows you to sample local varietals and learn about the winemaking process from informed specialists. It's a picturesque and delectable event, set against a backdrop of rolling vine-covered hills.

- **Cultural Events and Harvest Festivals:** Spring and autumn are prime times for cultural events and harvest festivals in Český Krumlov and the surrounding region. There are several possibilities to immerse yourself in local culture and cuisine, ranging from traditional folk events that celebrate Czech customs and traditions to food and wine festivals that highlight the wealth of the season.

Winter (December - February).

Český Krumlov becomes a fairytale-like landscape throughout the winter months. The snow-covered rooftops, dazzling lights, and warm atmosphere make it a lovely time to visit for people who don't mind the cold.

Český Krumlov has lots to see and do during the winter months, despite certain sites having limited hours or being closed for the season. The castle and ancient city center take on a peaceful air, and you may warm up with a cup of mulled wine or hot chocolate at one of the many cafes and restaurants.

Winter also presents unique activities such as ice skating on the frozen pond in the castle gardens or riding a horse-drawn sleigh through the snow-covered landscape. If you're lucky, you might be able to enjoy Český Krumlov covered in snow, producing a stunning winter paradise that's absolutely unforgettable.

Activities that can be done

- **Christmas Markets and Festive Traditions:** Visit Český Krumlov's Christmas markets to shop for handmade presents, savor traditional Czech foods, and enjoy festive music and entertainment. Don't miss the magical ambiance of the town square, which is filled with thousands of dazzling lights and decorated for the holidays.

- **Ice Skating and Sleigh Rides:** Embrace the winter wonderland of Český Krumlov by gliding across the ice at the outdoor skating rink in the castle gardens. A horse-drawn sleigh ride through the snowy countryside is a romantic or family-friendly adventure that allows you to appreciate the picturesque beauty of the winter scenery.

- **Cozy Cafes and Fireside Dining:** Warm up from the cold with a cozy meal or hot drink at one of Český Krumlov's inviting cafes and restaurants. Snuggle up by the fireside with a cup of mulled wine or eat hearty Czech comfort foods such as goulash, dumplings, and roasted meats. It's the ideal way to relax after a day of winter activities.

Whether you like the hustle and bustle of summer, the peacefulness of spring and autumn, or the enchantment of winter, there is never a bad time to visit Český Krumlov. Each season brings its own set of attractions and experiences, guaranteeing that every visit to this wonderful city is unforgettable and magical.

Duration of Stay Recommendations

You're planning a trip to Český Krumlov and are wondering how long to stay. Well, the longer the better! But, of course, not everyone has unlimited vacation time, so let us break it down.

- **Day Trip:** If you're short on time but still want to experience the magic of Český Krumlov, a day trip is certainly feasible. However, keep in mind that you'll just scratch the surface of everything this lovely town has to offer. With only a day, you'll most likely concentrate on the main sights, such as the castle, historic town, and perhaps a leisurely stroll along the Vltava River. While it is possible to visit the highlights in one day, you will most certainly be left wanting more.

- **Two to Three Days:** Okay, now we're talking! This is the sweet spot for experiencing Český Krumlov in all its glory. With two to three days, you'll have plenty of time to explore the town at your leisure, learn more about its history and culture, and even journey into the surrounding countryside. Spend your days strolling the cobblestone streets, enjoying the architecture, and stopping at small stores and cafes. Remember to schedule time for guided tours of the castle and other sights, as well as outdoor activities such as rafting or hiking. With a few nights in town, you'll have the opportunity to sample the local nightlife and even see a show at the Baroque theater. Spending two to three days in Český Krumlov will leave you with a sense of having thoroughly explored the city.

- **Extended Stay:** Now, if you have the luxury of time, why not extend your stay in Český Krumlov? A week or more of immersion allows for a more in-depth understanding of the local culture and lifestyle. Use this time to slow down and appreciate the small things - eat leisurely at charming eateries, strike up talks with locals, and see off-the-beaten-path sights. Český Krumlov serves as a base for exploring adjacent cities and attractions, including the medieval town of České Budějovice and the breathtaking Šumava National Park. Staying in Český Krumlov for a lengthy period of time allows you to become a part of the community and may even make it difficult to leave.

Here are the recommended stay durations for Český Krumlov. Whether you visit for a day trip or a longer holiday, Český Krumlov will leave you wanting more. So pack your luggage, reserve your accommodations, and prepare for an incredible vacation in this charming Czech town!

Weather and Climate Information

Český Krumlov has a temperate climate with four distinct seasons, each giving unique beauty and chances for adventure.

- **Spring (April to May):**

Springtime in Český Krumlov brings the awakening of nature, with trees budding, flowers blooming, and the landscape coming alive with vibrant colors. During this season, temperatures average between 10°C and 15°C (50°F to 59°F). While there may be occasional showers, the overall weather is nice and ideal for outdoor activities like walking tours, hiking, and seeing the city's beautiful gardens.

- **Summer (June to August):**

Summer is the peak tourist season in Český Krumlov, thanks to its warm temperatures and long days of sunshine. The average temperature during this period ranges from 20°C to 25°C (68°F to 77°F), making it ideal for sightseeing, river rafting, and outdoor festivities. However, it is worth mentioning that summer brings a lot of visitors, so be prepared for crowded attractions and higher hotel prices. To protect yourself from the sun's rays, remember to take sunscreen, sunglasses, and a hat.

- **Autumn (September to October):**

As summer transitions into autumn, Český Krumlov takes on a new beauty as the foliage begins to change colors, painting the landscape in shades of red, orange, and gold. Temperatures begin to cool, with averages ranging from 10°C to 15°C (50°F to 59°F), making it ideal for exploring the city on foot or taking leisurely bike rides along the Vltava River. Autumn also offers less crowds than the summer months, allowing for a more leisurely and personal experience.

- **Winter (December to February):**

Winter in Český Krumlov is a magical time, with snow-covered rooftops, cozy cafes, and the festive atmosphere of the holiday season. While temperatures can dip to between -5°C and 5°C (23°F and 41°F), the chilly weather is ideal for activities such as ice skating, sledding, and enjoying the town's Christmas markets. Keep in mind that some attractions may have reduced hours or close throughout the winter, so check ahead of time and prepare appropriately. To keep comfortable in the cold, remember to bundle up with thick layers, a hat, gloves, and sturdy boots.

Additional weather tips:

- **Rainfall:** While Český Krumlov experiences relatively consistent rainfall throughout the year, the months of May and June tend to be the wettest. Make sure to bring an umbrella or waterproof garment, especially if you're going during these months.

- **Altitude:** Český Krumlov sits at an elevation of approximately 492 meters (1,614 feet) above sea level. While this may not seem noteworthy, it's worth mentioning that higher altitudes might result in cooler temperatures and faster weather changes, so be prepared for unpredictable conditions during your visit.

Understanding the weather patterns and temperature of Český Krumlov can help guests plan their activities and pack appropriately for a comfortable and pleasurable stay in this picturesque Czech town. Český Krumlov has something for everyone, no matter the season, whether it's seeing ancient landmarks, going on outdoor activities, or simply soaking up local culture.

How to Get There

Let's talk about getting to Český Krumlov! Whether you're coming from within the Czech Republic or abroad, there are several transportation options to consider.

By Air

While Český Krumlov doesn't have its own airport, there are several nearby airports that serve as entry points for travelers. The two main airports to consider are Prague's Václav Havel Airport and Vienna International Airport in Austria.

- **PRAGUE'S VÁCLAV HAVEL AIRPORT (PRG):**

Distance to Český Krumlov: Approximately 170 kilometers (105 miles).

Transport Options to Český Krumlov:

- **Bus:** Direct buses operate from Prague's main bus station, Florenc, to Český Krumlov. The journey takes around 3 to 4 hours, depending on traffic and stops.
- **Train:** You can take a train from Prague's main train station, Praha hlavní nádraží, to Český Krumlov via České Budějovice. The train journey takes approximately 3 to 4 hours.
- **Rental Car**: Renting a car at Prague Airport gives you the flexibility to explore Český Krumlov and its surrounding areas at your own pace. The drive takes around 2 to 3 hours, depending on traffic and road conditions.
- **Airport Facilities:** Prague Airport offers a wide range of facilities and services to ensure a comfortable travel experience. These include duty-free shops, restaurants and cafes, currency exchange offices, car rental agencies, and lounges.

Transportation from Prague Airport to City Center: The airport is well-connected to Prague's city center by public transportation, including buses, Airport Express buses, and taxis. The Airport Express bus provides a direct connection to Prague's main train station, making it convenient for travelers continuing their journey to Český Krumlov by train.

- **VIENNA INTERNATIONAL AIRPORT (VIE), AUSTRIA:**

Distance to Český Krumlov: Approximately 200 kilometers (124 miles).

Transport Options to Český Krumlov:

- **Train:** From Vienna Airport, take the City Airport Train (CAT) or the S-Bahn commuter train to Vienna's main train station, Wien Hauptbahnhof. From there, you can catch a train to Český Krumlov via České Budějovice. The total travel time is approximately 4 to 5 hours, including the transfer.
- **Bus:** Alternatively, you can take a bus from Vienna's Erdberg Bus Station to Český Krumlov.

The journey takes around 4 to 5 hours, depending on traffic and stops.
- **Rental Car:** Renting a car at Vienna Airport gives you the flexibility to drive to Český Krumlov at your own pace. The drive takes approximately 3 to 4 hours, depending on traffic and road conditions.
- **Airport Facilities:** Vienna Airport offers a wide range of amenities, including shops, restaurants and cafes, currency exchange offices, car rental agencies, and lounges. The airport also provides services such as baggage storage, luggage wrapping, and medical assistance.

Transportation from Vienna Airport to City Center: Vienna Airport is well-connected to the city center by various transportation options, including trains, buses, taxis, and rental cars. The City Airport Train (CAT) offers a direct connection to Vienna's city center, with a journey time of approximately 16 minutes to Wien Mitte station.

When planning your trip to Český Krumlov, consider factors such as travel time, cost, and convenience when choosing the best airport and transportation option for your journey. Safe travels!

By Train

Traveling by train is a scenic and comfortable way to reach Český Krumlov from major cities within the Czech Republic and neighboring countries. Here's what you need to know:

Traveling by train is a convenient and scenic way to reach Český Krumlov, offering travelers a comfortable journey with picturesque views of the Czech countryside along the way. Here's what you need to know about taking the train to Český Krumlov:

1. From Prague:

If you're starting your journey in Prague, you'll depart from the city's main train station, Praha hlavní nádraží (Prague Main Station). Located in the city center, Praha hlavní nádraží is easily accessible by public transportation, including metro, tram, and bus.

- **Train Options:** Several trains operate between Prague and Český Krumlov, with varying travel times and amenities. It's essential to choose the right train based on your preferences for comfort, speed, and budget.

- **Direct Trains:** Direct trains from Prague to Český Krumlov are available, offering a convenient and straightforward journey without the need for transfers. These trains typically take around 3 to 4 hours to reach Český Krumlov, with comfortable seating and onboard facilities such as restrooms and snack bars.

- **Connections:** If there are no direct trains available for your preferred departure time, you may need to take a connecting train with a transfer in České Budějovice. While this adds a bit of travel time to your journey, it still provides a scenic route through the Czech countryside and the opportunity to explore České Budějovice, known for its historic architecture and renowned Budweiser beer.

- **Ticketing and Reservations**: It's recommended to purchase your train tickets in advance, especially during peak travel seasons or holidays when trains may be busier than usual. Tickets can be bought online through the Czech Railways website or at the train station ticket counters. Seat reservations are optional but recommended for long-distance journeys, as they guarantee you a specific seat on the train and help ensure a more comfortable travel experience.

- **Timetable and Schedule:** Trains from Prague to Český Krumlov operate throughout the day, with multiple departures to choose from. It's advisable to check the train timetable in advance and plan your journey accordingly. Be sure to allow some flexibility in your schedule, as train delays or schedule changes can occur, especially during inclement weather or unforeseen circumstances.

- **Facilities and Amenities**: Most trains traveling between Prague and Český Krumlov are equipped with modern amenities to enhance your travel experience. These may include comfortable seating with ample legroom, air conditioning or heating, onboard restrooms, and food and beverage services. Some trains also offer free Wi-Fi connectivity, allowing you to stay connected during your journey.

- **Scenic Views:** One of the highlights of traveling by train to Český Krumlov is the breathtaking scenery along the way. As you depart from Prague, you'll journey through the picturesque countryside of Bohemia, passing verdant forests, rolling hills, and charming villages. Keep your camera handy to capture the beauty of the landscape as it unfolds outside your window.

- **Arrival in Český Krumlov:** Upon arrival at Český Krumlov's train station, you'll find yourself just a short distance from the town center. From the station, you can easily reach your accommodation by walking, taking a taxi, or using public transportation. The walk from the train station to the town center takes approximately 15 to 20 minutes, allowing you to soak in the atmosphere of Český Krumlov as you make your way to your hotel or guesthouse.

2. From Vienna:

If you're starting your journey in Vienna, you have several options for traveling by train to Český Krumlov. While there are no direct trains from Vienna to Český Krumlov, you can take a combination of trains with transfers in České

Budějovice or Český Krumlov. Here's what you need to know:

- **Train Options:** The most common route from Vienna to Český Krumlov involves taking a train from Vienna to České Budějovice, then transferring to a connecting train or bus to Český Krumlov. While this route requires a transfer, it still provides a scenic journey through the Austrian and Czech countryside, with opportunities to admire the landscapes along the way.

From Vienna to České Budějovice: Trains from Vienna to České Budějovice depart from Vienna's main train station, Wien Hauptbahnhof (Vienna Central Station). The journey takes approximately 2 to 3 hours, depending on the type of train and any connections. Be sure to check the train timetable in advance and consider booking your tickets online to secure your preferred departure time.

- **From České Budějovice to Český Krumlov:** Upon arrival in České Budějovice, you'll need to transfer to a connecting train or bus to reach Český Krumlov. The train station in České

Budějovice is located within walking distance of the city center, making it easy to navigate. From there, you can catch a train or bus to Český Krumlov, with travel times ranging from 45 minutes to 1 hour.

- **Ticketing and Reservations:** Similar to traveling from Prague, it's recommended to purchase your train tickets in advance, especially during peak travel seasons or holidays. Tickets can be bought online through the Austrian Federal Railways (ÖBB) website or at the train station ticket counters. Seat reservations are optional but recommended for long-distance journeys, as they ensure you have a specific seat on the train and help guarantee a more comfortable travel experience.

- **Timetable and Schedule:** Trains from Vienna to České Budějovice operate throughout the day, with multiple departures to choose from. Be sure to check the train timetable in advance and plan your journey accordingly. Keep in mind that there may be limited options for connecting trains or buses from České Budějovice to Český Krumlov, so it's essential to coordinate your travel plans accordingly.

- **Facilities and Amenities:** Trains traveling from Vienna to České Budějovice are equipped with modern amenities to ensure a comfortable journey. These may include comfortable seating, air conditioning or heating, onboard restrooms, and food and beverage services. Some trains also offer free Wi-Fi connectivity, allowing you to stay connected during your journey.

- **Scenic Views:** As you depart from Vienna and make your way through the Austrian and Czech countryside, you'll be treated to stunning views of rolling hills, picturesque villages, and lush greenery. Keep your camera handy to capture the beauty of the landscape as it unfolds outside your window, and don't forget to take advantage of photo opportunities during your journey.

- **Arrival in Český Krumlov:** Upon arrival in Český Krumlov, you'll find yourself at the town's train or bus station, depending on your mode of transportation. From there, you can easily reach the town center and your accommodation by walking, taking a taxi, or using public transportation. The walk from the train station to the town center takes approximately 15 to 20 minutes, allowing you to soak in the atmosphere of Český Krumlov as you make your way to your hotel or guesthouse.

Traveling by train to Český Krumlov offers a convenient and enjoyable way to experience the beauty of the Czech Republic's countryside while making your way to this enchanting medieval town. Sit back, relax, and enjoy the journey as you embark on your Český Krumlov adventure by train!

By Bus

Buses are a popular and convenient mode of transportation for travelers heading to Český Krumlov, offering direct routes from Prague and other major cities within the Czech Republic. Here's everything you need to know about traveling by bus:

From Prague:
Buses from Prague to Český Krumlov depart from the city's main bus station, Florenc. This station is centrally located and easily accessible via public transportation or taxi. It's recommended to purchase your bus tickets in advance, especially

during peak tourist seasons, to secure your seat and avoid last-minute hassles.

- **Bus Companies:** Several bus companies operate routes between Prague and Český Krumlov, including Student Agency, RegioJet, and FlixBus. Each company offers multiple departures throughout the day, providing travelers with flexibility in choosing their preferred departure time.

- **Travel Time:** The journey from Prague to Český Krumlov by bus typically takes around 3 to 4 hours, depending on traffic and any scheduled stops along the way. The route offers scenic views of the Czech countryside, making the travel time feel shorter and more enjoyable.

- **Ticket Booking:** Tickets for buses can be purchased online through the respective bus company's website or at the ticket counters in Prague's main bus station, Florenc. Online booking is recommended for added convenience and peace of mind, as popular departure times may sell out quickly.

- **Onboard Amenities:** Most buses traveling between Prague and Český Krumlov are equipped with modern amenities to ensure a comfortable journey. These may include comfortable seating, air conditioning, onboard restrooms, Wi-Fi, and entertainment options such as movies or music.

- **Luggage Allowance:** Bus companies typically have specific policies regarding luggage allowance and restrictions. It's important to familiarize yourself with these policies before traveling to ensure a hassle-free experience. Additionally, larger items such as bicycles or oversized luggage may require additional fees or special arrangements.

- **Arrival in Český Krumlov:** Buses arriving in Český Krumlov typically drop off passengers at the town's main bus station, which is conveniently located within walking distance of the historic city center. From the bus station, it's a short stroll to popular attractions, accommodations, restaurants, and shops.

From Other Cities:

In addition to Prague, Český Krumlov is also accessible by bus from other major cities within the Czech Republic, such as Brno, České Budějovice, and

Plzeň. These routes may vary in frequency and travel time depending on the distance and popularity of the destination. Travelers can check the schedules and book tickets through the respective bus company's website or at local ticket offices.

Traveling to Český Krumlov by bus offers convenience, affordability, and the opportunity to enjoy scenic views of the Czech countryside along the way. Whether you're coming from Prague or other cities within the country, buses provide a comfortable and efficient mode of transportation for your journey to this enchanting destination.

By Car

Renting a car is a fantastic option for travelers who prefer flexibility and independence when exploring Český Krumlov and its surrounding areas. Here's everything you need to know about traveling to Český Krumlov by car:

Route from Prague:

The most common route from Prague to Český Krumlov is via the D1/E55 highway south towards České Budějovice. This highway offers a smooth and scenic drive through the picturesque Czech countryside.

After passing through České Budějovice, you'll continue on the E55 towards Český Krumlov. Keep an eye out for signs directing you to the town center.

The total driving distance from Prague to Český Krumlov is approximately 170 kilometers, and the journey takes around 2 to 3 hours, depending on traffic and road conditions.

Along the way, you'll pass through charming towns and villages, providing opportunities to stop and stretch your legs, grab a snack, or snap some photos of the scenic landscapes.

Route from Vienna:

If you're traveling from Vienna, you'll take the A22 and E59 highways north towards České Budějovice. This route offers a scenic drive through the Austrian and Czech countryside.

After crossing the border into the Czech Republic, you'll continue on the E59 towards České Budějovice and then follow signs for Český Krumlov.

The total driving distance from Vienna to Český Krumlov is approximately 200 kilometers, and the journey takes around 3 to 4 hours, depending on traffic and border crossings.

Be sure to have your passport and any required documents ready for border control when crossing into the Czech Republic.

Parking in Český Krumlov:

Once you arrive in Český Krumlov, you'll need to find parking, especially if your accommodation doesn't offer on-site parking.

Parking in the historic center of Český Krumlov is limited and can be quite expensive. There are several paid parking lots available, including P1, P2, and P3, located just outside the town center.

It's recommended to park your car in one of these designated parking lots and explore Český Krumlov on foot. The town center is pedestrian-friendly, and most of the major attractions are within walking distance.

Driving Tips:

- Before hitting the road, familiarize yourself with Czech traffic rules and regulations. Speed limits, road signs, and driving etiquette may differ from what you're used to in your home country.
- Keep in mind that some roads in rural areas may be narrow and winding, so drive cautiously and be aware of other vehicles, pedestrians, and cyclists sharing the road.
- If you're traveling during the winter months, be prepared for potentially hazardous driving conditions, including snow, ice, and reduced visibility. Make sure your rental car is equipped with winter tires and carry snow chains for added safety.

Traveling to Český Krumlov by car allows you to explore the beautiful Czech countryside at your own pace and discover hidden gems along the way. Just remember to plan your route in advance, drive safely, and enjoy the journey!

Visa and Entry Requirements

- **Schengen Area:** Český Krumlov is located in the Czech Republic, which is a member of the Schengen Area. Travelers from Schengen Area nations do not require a visa to visit the Czech Republic for short stays of up to 90 days within a 180-day period.

- **Visa-Free Entry:** Many nations, including the United States, Canada, Australia, and most European countries, do not require a visa for short-term tourist or business trips to the Czech Republic. They can enter the nation without a visa for periods of up to 90 days within a 180-day window.

- **Visa Requirements:** Depending on their nationality and the purpose of their stay, visitors from countries outside the Schengen Area may be required to obtain a visa before entering the Czech Republic. Visa requirements differ according to the traveler's country of citizenship, duration of stay, and proposed activity.

- **Visas:** The Czech Republic provides a variety of visas, including tourist, business, student, and work visas. Travelers should apply for the proper visa for their anticipated activity while in the nation.

- **Application Process:** To apply for a visa to the Czech Republic, travelers typically need to submit a visa application form, a valid passport, passport-sized photos, proof of travel insurance, proof of accommodation, and evidence of sufficient funds to cover their stay. Additional documents may be required, depending on the type of visa and the traveler's specific circumstances.

- **Visa Application Centers:** Visa applications are typically processed at Czech embassies or consulates in the traveler's home country. Some nations also have visa application facilities where visitors can submit their applications in person or electronically.

- **Processing Time:** The processing time for visa applications varies by nation and visa category. Travelers should apply for their visas well in advance of their scheduled travel dates to allow for adequate processing time.

- **Border Control:** Upon arrival in the Czech Republic, visitors may be subjected to border control checks by immigration officers. They may be asked to show their passport, visa (if applicable), return or onward travel itinerary, and proof of adequate cash for their stay.

- **Length of Stay:** Tourists and other short-term visitors are typically allowed to stay in the Czech Republic for up to 90 days within a 180-day period without a visa. Travelers who want to stay longer or engage in activities like employment or study may need to apply for a long-term visa or residency permit.

Before arranging a trip to Český Krumlov, travelers should check their nationality's unique visa requirements and entrance laws. This can be accomplished by visiting the website of the nearest Czech embassy or consulate, or by contacting the Czech Ministry of Foreign Affairs for help. Visiting Český Krumlov and the Czech Republic can be hassle-free if visa and entry formalities are met.

Chapter 2

TOP TOURIST ATTRACTIONS

Welcome to the heart of Český Krumlov, where every corner tells a story and every cobblestone whispers centuries of secrets. Prepare to embark on a journey through time as we discover the top tourist attractions that make this lovely Czech town a fascinating vacation.

Český Krumlov Castle.

As you approach Český Krumlov Castle, prepare to be taken back in time to the height of the Renaissance. The castle's beautiful façade, which towers over the town, reflects centuries of history, art, and culture. Originally built in the 13th century by the strong Rosenberg family, the castle was extensively renovated in the 16th and 17th centuries, making it into the architectural masterpiece we see today.

Castle Museum: Discovering Treasures from the Past

Explore the Castle Museum and learn about Český Krumlov's fascinating history. The museum, located within the castle's labyrinthine corridors, houses a vast collection of relics dating back over 700 years. Each chamber in Český Krumlov reflects the rich lifestyle of its noble residents, with beautifully carved furniture and rare artworks by renowned masters.

Baroque Theater: A Stage Fit for Royalty.

The Baroque Theater at Český Krumlov Castle is a must-see for any visitor. Built in the 17th century and scrupulously kept to this day, the theater exemplifies the grandeur of European performing art. Take a guided walk into the theater's opulent interior, which is equipped with exquisite stage machinery, ornate costumes, and intricate scenery. If you're lucky, you might even witness a live performance or historical recreation during your stay.

Castle Gardens is a tranquil oasis.

After visiting the castle's sumptuous interiors, take a leisurely stroll through the beautiful Castle Gardens. These finely maintained gardens, spanning 11 hectares, provide a tranquil escape from the rush and activity of the town below. As you walk down winding roads surrounded with ancient trees, you will notice groomed lawns, vibrant flower beds, and tranquil ponds. Climb the Castle Tower to see panoramic views of Český Krumlov and the surrounding landscape.

Events and Festivals: Celebrating Culture and Heritage

Český Krumlov Castle hosts annual events and festivals that highlight the town's cultural heritage. From medieval jousting battles to classical music performances, there's always something fascinating going on inside the castle walls. Check the castle's official website or local event listings to see what's going on during your stay, and get ready to immerse yourself in the vivid tapestry of Czech culture.

Practical Information: Tips for Visitors

Here are some helpful recommendations to make your visit to Český Krumlov Castle more enjoyable:

- **Opening Hours:** The castle is usually open to tourists from the morning until early evening, but hours may change depending on the season.
- **Guided Tours:** Consider joining a guided tour to make the most of your visit and gain insights into the castle's history and architecture.
- **Ticket Information:** Admission tickets can be purchased on-site or online in advance to prevent long lines, particularly during high tourist season.
- **Accessibility:** While the majority of the castle is accessible to guests with mobility challenges, some sections may have steps or uneven surfaces, so plan appropriately.

Český Krumlov Castle, known for its rich history, spectacular architecture, and breathtaking views, is a must-see attraction in this picturesque Czech town. So don't pass up the opportunity to travel back in time and experience the enchantment of this historic landmark firsthand!

Historic City Center

Welcome to the heart of Český Krumlov, where every cobblestone tells a story of centuries past and each building whispers secrets of medieval greatness. When you enter the Historic City Center, you will feel as if you have gone back in time to a realm straight out of a fairytale.

- **Architectural marvels:**

The Historic City Center is a UNESCO World Heritage Site known for its beautiful architecture, which combines Gothic, Renaissance, and Baroque styles. Take a leisurely stroll through the labyrinthine lanes, admiring the elaborate façade of centuries-old buildings embellished with bright murals, decorative gables, and graceful arcades. Look up and enjoy the skyline's soaring spires and stately towers, which provide breathtaking views of the surrounding area.

- **Town Square:**

The bustling Town Square, located in the heart of the Historic City Center, is a thriving hub of activity where both locals and visitors meet to enjoy the lively environment. Surrounded by attractive cafes, small boutiques, and picturesque townhouses, the square is the ideal place to unwind and people-watch while sipping on a cup of freshly brewed coffee or indulging in a delectable pastry. Don't miss the chance to photograph the iconic Plague Column, a remarkable monument symbolizing the town's perseverance in the face of hardship.

- **Hidden Gems:**

One of the highlights of exploring the Historic City Center is discovering hidden gems buried away in quiet corners and isolated courtyards. Keep an eye out for tucked-away artisan studios, quaint boutiques selling locally crafted products, and snug wine cellars drinking velvety Moravian wine. Wander off the usual road to find hidden alleys dotted with blossoming flowers, medieval wells, and whimsical sculptures that contribute to the area's wonderful atmosphere.

- **Cultural landmarks:**

The Historic City Center features cultural landmarks that showcase Český Krumlov's rich legacy. Visit the Minorite Monastery, a peaceful refuge amidst the rush and bustle of the town center. Explore the monastery's tranquil courtyard and enjoy its magnificent Baroque architecture before venturing inside to uncover its hidden treasures, which include ancient manuscripts, holy items, and breathtaking frescos.

- **Local cuisine:**

No trip to the Historic City Center is complete without trying the wonderful flavors of Czech cuisine. From substantial goulash and crispy schnitzel to delicious dumplings and creamy Czech cheeses, the town's restaurants and pubs serve a delectable selection of traditional cuisine that will delight every appetite. Wash it all down with a glass of locally brewed beer or a shot of flaming Slivovitz, a traditional Czech plum brandy.

- **Evening entertainment:**

As the sun sets and the stars appear, the Historic City Center comes alive with a thriving nightlife scene. Join the locals at one of the town's cozy pubs or wine bars and enjoy live music, folk dancing, and impromptu jam sessions that celebrate Český Krumlov's rich cultural heritage. Or, for a more refined evening out, attend a performance at one of the town's ancient theaters or concert halls, where you can enjoy classical music, opera, and theater shows in a beautiful setting.

Discover Český Krumlov's Historic City Center, rich in history, culture, and culinary pleasures. So put on your walking shoes, take your camera, and prepare to embark on a journey through time in this enchanting Czech town!

Egon Schiele Art Centrum

The Egon Schiele Art Centrum, located in the historic city of Český Krumlov, is a must-see for expressionist art enthusiasts. This cultural institution is named for the renowned Austrian painter Egon Schiele and commemorates his life, works, and influence on modern art.

Upon entering the Art Centrum, visitors are met by a compelling collection of Schiele's paintings, drawings, and prints, which have been carefully curated to provide insight into the artist's turbulent life and innovative artistic vision. From his early investigations of the human form to his later experiments with color and abstraction, the displays provide a complete overview of Schiele's changing style and topics.

In addition to Schiele's own works, the Art Centrum organizes temporary exhibitions of works by other famous expressionist painters, giving visitors a larger context for understanding Schiele's place in the art world. These rotating displays highlight the range and energy of early twentieth-century European art, allowing visitors to explore new artists and trends alongside Schiele's classic works.

However, the Egon Schiele Art Centrum is more than just a gallery; it is a center for artistic production and instruction. Throughout the year, the Centrum hosts a variety of events, such as lectures, workshops, and guided tours, designed to engage people of all ages and backgrounds. Whether you are a seasoned art enthusiast or a curious newbie, the Art Centrum has something for everyone to enjoy and learn from.

After immersing yourself in Schiele's universe, take a minute to unwind and think in the Centrum's quiet garden, a serene sanctuary situated amid the hectic city core. Surrounded by lush greenery and aromatic flowers, this hidden gem is ideal for calm reflection and inspiration.

Before you depart, stop by the Centrum's gift store, where you can explore a handpicked variety of art books, posters, and souvenirs inspired by Schiele's legendary work. Whether you're looking for a souvenir of your trip or a one-of-a-kind gift for a fellow art enthusiast, you'll discover something special to treasure.

Finally, the Egon Schiele Art Centrum in Český Krumlov provides a unique opportunity to learn about one of the 20th century's most influential artists. It's a must-see place for anybody interested in art and culture, thanks to its thought-provoking exhibits, interesting activities, and tranquil surroundings.

Český Krumlov Regional Museum

The Český Krumlov Regional Museum, located in a historic building overlooking the gorgeous Vltava River, provides visitors with a mesmerizing trip through the town's rich and diversified legacy. The museum exhibits present a thorough account of Český Krumlov's progress over centuries, including archeological relics, folk traditions, medieval craftsmanship, and current advancements.

Highlights of Museum

Upon entering the museum, you will be greeted by a broad assortment of exhibitions spread across many floors and galleries. Here are some of the highlights you shouldn't miss:

- **Archaeological Discoveries:** Explore Český Krumlov's ancient past through a fascinating collection of archaeological finds. From Neolithic implements to Roman artifacts, these remnants provide vital information about the region's early people and their way of life.

- **Medieval Crafts and Trades:** Learn about the tools and techniques used by craftsmen and artisans in Český Krumlov. Marvel at elaborately created metalwork, delicate fabrics, and gorgeous pottery, all of which demonstrate the skill and inventiveness of previous generations.

- **Folk Traditions and Customs:** Immerse yourself in the vibrant tapestry of Český Krumlov's folk traditions and customs. From bright costumes to energetic music and dance, the museum honors the region's rich cultural heritage while also providing significant insights into their daily lives and celebrations.

- **Baroque Splendor:** Journey through the opulent world of the Baroque era as you admire exquisite furniture, fine art, and ornate decorations from Český Krumlov's golden age. Highlights include breathtaking examples of Baroque sculpture, art, and architecture, all scrupulously conserved for future generations to appreciate.

- **Modern Exhibits:** Explore modern themes and concerns affecting Český Krumlov and its citizens through thought-provoking and interactive displays. From environmental conservation to urban development, these exhibits offer a fresh perspective on the challenges and opportunities facing this historic town in the 21st century.

Guided Tours and Educational Programs

Consider taking a guided tour of the museum's collections and themes, which will provide you with a better understanding of them. These tours provide useful insights and context, helping you to fully comprehend the relevance of each exhibit.

Additionally, the museum provides a variety of educational activities and workshops for visitors of all ages. These programs, which range from hands-on craft activities to scholarly lectures, offer fascinating possibilities for learning and exploration.

Practical information.

Before visiting the Český Krumlov Regional Museum, here are some practical advice to maximize your experience.

- **Opening Hours:** For information about museum hours and special events, see their website or contact them directly.
- **Tickets and Admission:** Buy your tickets in advance whenever possible to prevent long lines, especially during busy tourist seasons.
- **Accessibility:** The museum is wheelchair accessible, with elevators and ramps provided for those with mobility issues.
- **Photography and Filming:** Follow any prohibitions on photography and filming within the museum, and be considerate of other visitors.

The Český Krumlov Regional Museum provides a captivating tour through the history, culture, and traditions of this charming Czech town. Whether you're a history buff, art enthusiast, or simply interested about the world around you, a visit to the museum will improve your experience and deepen your appreciation for Český Krumlov's distinct identity. So don't pass up this chance to discover the past and present of one of Europe's most popular attractions!

St. Vitus Church

Explore Český Krumlov's religious sites, including the St. Vitus Church, which is a must-see for all visitors. As you approach St. Vitus Church, you'll be captivated by its magnificent Gothic façade, which is embellished with beautiful stone carvings and delicate spires reaching for the sky. This architectural masterpiece from the 15th century showcases the religious commitment and artistic competence of Český Krumlov's former people.

When you walk inside, you'll be met by a sanctuary of unparalleled beauty and peace. St. Vitus Church's interior is a sensory delight, with soaring vaulted ceilings, graceful arches, and a plethora of breathtaking religious artwork. Take a minute to study the amazing stained glass windows, which flood the chamber with kaleidoscope colors of light, generating a sense of holy awe.

As you investigate more, you'll come across a wealth of religious objects and historical relics. Admire the beautiful altars covered with intricate woodcarvings and gilded ornaments, each one a tribute to the artistry of previous generations. Don't miss the opportunity to explore the church's greatest items, including rare paintings, sculptures, and sacred relics that offer insight into Český Krumlov's spiritual legacy.

For those interested in the church's history, guided tours are provided, which provide detailed information about the church's significance and architectural aspects. Discover St. Vitus, the church's patron saint, and his impact on Český Krumlov's religious traditions. Discover the stories behind the church's building and renovation efforts, which have kept it beautiful for centuries.

In addition to its liturgical significance, St. Vitus Church hosts cultural events and concerts year-round. Keep a watch out for exceptional events and musical recitals presented within the church's hallowed walls, where the acoustics accentuate the beauty of the music and provide an unforgettable experience.

Before you go, take a minute to meditate in the peaceful sanctuary of St. Vitus Church. Whether you're looking for spiritual comfort, artistic inspiration, or simply a moment of calm during your travels, this hallowed sanctuary provides a welcome break from the outside world.

When visiting Český Krumlov, don't miss out on visiting St. Vitus Church. Its timeless beauty and spiritual elegance will fascinate you.

Český Krumlov Baroque Theater

xxEnter the Český Krumlov Baroque Theater to experience the golden age of European theater. Built in the 17th century and scrupulously kept till now, this ancient theater provides tourists with a rare view into the sumptuous world of Baroque performing art.

History & Architecture

As you enter the theater, take a time to appreciate the wonderful building, which embodies the grandeur and beauty of the Baroque period. The theater's beautifully adorned interior boasts intricate woodwork, opulent gilding, and gorgeous velvet drapes, resulting in a really magnificent spectacle.

Stage machinery

The Český Krumlov Baroque Theater boasts unique stage machinery that is still in use today. Admire the elaborate system of pulleys, levers, and ropes that enables for flawless scene transitions and extraordinary effects like flying angels and booming storms. During guided tours, knowledgeable docents will illustrate how the stage apparatus works, providing a behind-the-scenes glimpse into the wonder of Baroque theater.

Costumes and Props

The Český Krumlov Baroque Theater boasts an impressive collection of period costumes and props. From magnificent ball gowns to exquisite masks, the theater's costume department is a treasure trove of clothing that formerly adorned the stage in opulent shows. Visitors can also see the intricately constructed props, which range from exquisite swords to delicate hand-painted backgrounds and transport audiences to other locations and bygone ages.

Performances and Events

Although the Český Krumlov Baroque Theater no longer holds regular performances, it nevertheless accommodates special events and productions throughout the year. Baroque operas and classical concerts, as well as dramatic reenactments and historical pageants, provide guests with a one-of-a-kind opportunity to experience the magic of the theater in its original setting. Check the theater's schedule of events to see what's going on during your visit.

Guided tours

To fully appreciate the beauty and history of the Český Krumlov Baroque Theater, consider joining a guided tour with qualified professionals. During these excursions, you'll learn about the theater's interesting history, its significance to Czech cultural heritage, and the precise craftsmanship that went into its building and upkeep. Guides will also tell you stories about the theater's rich history, from royal performances to backstage intrigue.

Visitor Information

The Český Krumlov Baroque Theater is open year-round and offers guided tours in many languages. Tickets can be purchased on-site or in advance online, and discounts are frequently available for students, seniors, and organizations. The theater is wheelchair accessible, and special accommodations are given for disabled people. Photography is permitted during guided tours, so make sure to catch the magic of this ancient site on camera.

The Český Krumlov Baroque Theater transports visitors back to a time of elegance, extravagance, and artistic excellence. Whether you're a history buff, a theatrical fan, or just an inquisitive traveler, this fascinating cultural gem promises an amazing experience that will captivate you. Experience the magic of the Baroque era at the Český Krumlov Baroque Theater!

Vltava River Rafting and Canoeing

Picture this: you're gliding down the crystal-clear waters of the Vltava River, surrounded by lush greenery and towering cliffs that seem to touch the sky. The sun is shining, the birds are chirping, and you are in complete joy as you negotiate the calm currents of one of Europe's most gorgeous waterways.

Rafting and canoeing on the Vltava River is a must-do activity for outdoor enthusiasts and nature lovers in Český Krumlov. Whether you're an experienced paddler or a beginner seeking for a new adventure, there are alternatives for every skill level.

Choosing Your Adventure

Before you go on your river adventure, you must pick whether you want to go rafting or canoeing. Rafting is ideal for groups and families because you will paddle together in a huge inflatable raft accompanied by an expert instructor. Canoeing, on the other hand, provides a more private experience, allowing you to paddle at your own pace in a smaller watercraft with one or two other people.

Route Options

There are various routes accessible for Vltava River rafting and canoeing, each with its own distinct scenery and level of difficulty. The most popular route for beginners and families is the segment of the river that runs from Český Krumlov to Zlatá Koruna, a gorgeous stretch of water with gentle rapids and stunning natural vistas.

For experienced paddlers looking for a challenge, the river between Zlatá Koruna and České Budějovice offers faster currents and small rapids to traverse. This route takes you through picturesque scenery filled with attractive villages and historic landmarks, allowing plenty possibilities for exploring along the way.

Guided Tours vs. Self-Guided Excursions

If you're new to river rafting or canoeing, you might feel more at ease attending a guided tour lead by professional instructors who will teach you about safety, paddling skills, and local knowledge. Guided trips usually include all essential equipment, such as rafts, paddles, life jackets, and waterproof bags for your valuables.

Self-guided tours are also available for more experienced paddlers who prefer to explore the river on their own. Keep in mind that self-guided expeditions necessitate meticulous preparation and navigation skills, as well as a fundamental awareness of river safety standards.

What to bring.

Before embarking on your Vltava River journey, make sure you pack correctly for the day on the river. Essentials include:

- Sunscreen and sun hat to protect against UV rays
- Waterproof clothing and footwear.
- Snacks and plenty of water to stay hydrated
- Waterproof camera or smartphone to capture the breathtaking scenery
- First aid kit and emergency contact information
- Trash bags to pack out any waste and help preserve the pristine beauty of the river Safety Considerations

While Vltava River rafting and canoeing provide an excellent opportunity to reconnect with nature, it is critical to emphasize safety at all times. Make sure to:

- Always wear a properly fitted life jacket while out on the water.
- Pay attention to your guide's advice and obey all safety precautions.
- Stay attentive and aware of your surroundings, particularly in places with swift currents or barriers.
- Avoid consuming alcohol before or during your river trip.
- Check the weather forecast and river conditions before leaving, and be ready to postpone or cancel your excursion if conditions are unsafe.

Following these suggestions and instructions will ensure a safe and memorable Vltava River rafting or canoeing adventure in Český Krumlov. So take your paddle, enjoy the adventure, and let the beauty of the river lead you on an incredible voyage into the heart of Bohemia!

Brewery Tours

In Český Krumlov, beer is not just a beverage – it's a way of life. The town has a long and proud tradition of brewing, dating back to medieval times. Today, guests can walk behind the scenes and see the beauty and workmanship that goes into each pint of Czech beer.

Local breweries

First, let's discuss the breweries you may visit in Český Krumlov. While the town is small, it is home to multiple breweries, each with their own distinct flavor and brewing style. Some of the most popular breweries to visit are:

- **Eggenberg Brewery:** Situated just a stone's throw from Český Krumlov Castle, Eggenberg Brewery is one of the oldest and most esteemed breweries in the region. This ancient brewery, founded in the 16th century, produces classic Czech beers such as pilsners, lagers, and dark ales.
Address: Latrán 27, 381-01 Český Krumlov, Czech Republic.

- **Pivovar Krumlov:** Located in the heart of the Old Town, Pivovar Krumlov is a microbrewery known for its innovative approach to brewing. You can sample a selection of small-batch beers made with both traditional and modern processes. Don't miss the brewery's seasonal brews, which highlight the master brewers' originality and talent.
Address: Kájovská 55, 381-01 Český Krumlov, Czech Republic.

- **Pivovar Eggenberg:** Not to be confused with Eggenberg Brewery, Pivovar Eggenberg is another popular destination for beer enthusiasts in Český Krumlov. This family-owned brewery takes pride in its commitment to quality and authenticity, creating a variety of traditional Czech beers that are popular with both residents and visitors.
Address: Masná 136, 381 01, Český Krumlov, Czech Republic.

Guided tours

Now you know where to go, let's speak about how to experience Český Krumlov's breweries fully.

Many breweries offer guided tours that give visitors a behind-the-scenes peek at the brewing process, from grain to glass. What to expect on a normal brewery tour:

- **Brewery History:** Discover Český Krumlov's centuries-long brewing tradition. Discover the fascinating histories of the town's most famous breweries and their contributions to Czech beer culture.

- **Brewing Process:** Get an inside look at the brewing process, from mashing and lautering to fermentation and conditioning. Watch professional brewers work their magic, transforming simple materials like malt, hops, water, and yeast into flavorful, aromatic beer.

- **Tasting Sessions:** No brewery tour is complete without a tasting session! Sample a variety of beers directly from the source, escorted by knowledgeable personnel who will explain the subtleties of each brew. From crisp, refreshing lagers to rich, nuanced ales, there's something for everyone's taste.

- **Beer Pairing:** Enhance your tasting experience with a beer pairing session, where you'll learn how to pair various beer styles with complementing flavors and meals. Learn how to match beer with cheese, chocolate, charcuterie, and other foods, and dazzle your friends with your newly acquired knowledge.

Practical Tips

Before embarking on a brewery tour, here are a few practical tips to consider:

- **Booking:** Many breweries demand advanced reservations for tours, particularly during peak tourist seasons. Check the brewery's website or contact them directly to reserve your slot.
- **Transportation:** Consider how you'll get to and from the brewery, especially if it's located outside the town center. Some breweries may provide shuttle services or guided tours with transportation.
- **Dress Code:** Comfortable shoes and attire suitable for walking and standing are recommended, as brewery tours frequently

require going through production facilities and tasting rooms.
- **Souvenirs:** Don't forget to pick up some souvenirs to commemorate your brewery tour experience! Many breweries include on-site shops where you may buy bottles of beer, glassware, merchandise, and other souvenirs.

Immerse yourself in the world of Czech beer through brewery tours in Český Krumlov. You'll develop a newfound respect for this beloved beverage and the workmanship that goes into its making. Celebrate an incredible tour through the cuisine and customs of Český Krumlov!

Bear Sanctuary

Last but not least, make sure to visit the Bear Sanctuary. Nestled in the calm forests of Český Krumlov is a unique sanctuary for rescued bears from captivity and mistreatment. The Bear Sanctuary, which was founded with the goal of providing a safe and natural home for these majestic creatures, provides visitors with a one-of-a-kind opportunity to watch bears in their natural habitat and learn about local wildlife conservation initiatives.

History & Mission

The Bear Sanctuary traces its beginnings to a terrible period in European bear exploitation history. Many of the bears housed here were previously kept in captivity in appalling conditions, forced to perform in circuses, roadside attractions, or as pets in private households. Recognizing the need for action, a committed team of conservationists and animal welfare campaigners banded together to rescue the bears and give them a second chance at life.

Facilities and Habitat

The Bear Sanctuary, which spans acres of lush forested terrain, provides adequate area for its members to wander, forage, and engage in natural behaviors. The enclosures are deliberately constructed to resemble the bears' natural habitat, replete with dens, climbing structures, and pools for swimming and cooling off during the warmer months. Visitors can watch the bears from approved viewing platforms located at strategic vantage points, minimizing disturbance to the animals.

Meet the bears.

Each bear at the sanctuary has a distinct story to tell, and visitors can learn about their respective backgrounds and personalities. The sanctuary is home to a diverse mix of Ursine inhabitants, including lively cubs and knowledgeable old bears, each with their own idiosyncrasies and preferences. Knowledgeable staff members are available to provide information about bear behavior, biology, and the issues they encounter in the wild.

Conservation & Education

Beyond providing a safe refuge for rescued bears, the sanctuary is critical in spreading awareness about wildlife conservation and the need of preserving bear populations in their natural habitats. Educational workshops and guided excursions allow visitors to have a better awareness of the difficulties that bears face in Europe and around the world, empowering them to become change agents.

Visitor Experience

A visit to the Bear Sanctuary is not only an opportunity to interact with nature and see the majesty of these wonderful creatures up close, but also to make a positive influence through responsible tourism. Visitors can help the sanctuary by making donations, purchasing items from the gift store, or just telling their friends and family about their experience.

Practical information.

- **Location:** The Bear Sanctuary is located a short drive from Český Krumlov, making it easily accessible for visitors.
- **Opening Hours:** The sanctuary is normally available to tourists all year, with hours varied depending on the season. To get the most up-to-date information, visit the official website or contact the sanctuary directly.
- **Admission:** Entry fees contribute to the care and maintenance of the bears and the operation of the sanctuary. Discounts may be available to children, seniors, and groups.
- **Guided Tours:** Guided tours given by knowledgeable staff members provide unique insights into the sanctuary's residents' lives as well as the conservation efforts underway.
- **Visitor guidelines:** To promote the safety and well-being of both visitors and bears, some guidelines may be in place, such as keeping a

respectful distance from the animals and abstaining from feeding or approaching them.

A visit to the Bear Sanctuary is not only a memorable experience, but also an important opportunity to help wildlife conservation efforts and improve the lives of rescued bears. So come, soak up the beauty of nature, and leave with a renewed appreciation for these incredible creatures.

Český Krumlov offers a unique experience for guests of all ages and interests. So grab your camera, lace up your walking shoes, and prepare to embark on the trip of a lifetime in this enchanting Czech town!

Chapter 3

WHAT TO DO AND NOT TO DO

Congratulations for making it to Český Krumlov! Now, let's speak about what you can do to make the most of your time here, as well as what you should avoid doing to ensure a positive and respectful experience.

Cultural Etiquette

Cultural etiquette in Český Krumlov is deeply rooted in Czech history and traditions. While exploring this picturesque village, you will come across several customs that highlight the local heritage. Dress modestly when visiting religious locations such as St. Vitus Church or the monastery to respect the holiness of the location. This includes covering your shoulders and knees and removing your caps as a symbol of respect.

When interacting with locals, a few courteous phrases in Czech can go a long way toward building goodwill. "Dobrý den" (good day) and "prosím" (please) are simple yet effective terms to demonstrate admiration for local culture. Furthermore, addressing people by their titles and surnames, particularly in formal contexts, is considered respectful. Addressing someone as "Paní Nováková" (Mrs. Nováková) or "Pan Novák" (Mr. Novák) shows respect.

When dining out, keep in mind that Czech meals are typically savored gradually, with a focus on mingling and appreciating each dish. It is usual to wait until everyone at the table has been served before beginning your dinner, and don't be shocked if the amounts are large; Czech cuisine is recognized for its robust and tasty meals. And, of course, leave a 10% tip for good service, since waitstaff appreciate it.

Respectful behavior toward locals.

Traveling to Český Krumlov provides an opportunity to meet with people and immerse yourself in the community. Český Krumlov is recognized for its friendly hospitality, and exhibiting respect and thoughtfulness will enhance your experience and leave a great impression.

When dealing with locals, a cheerful manner and genuine interest in their culture and traditions will be greatly appreciated. Whether you're conversing with a shopkeeper, eating at a local restaurant, or attending a cultural event, take the time to interact with others and learn about their experiences. A simple "Děkuji" (thank you) or "Na shledanou" (goodbye) in Czech can help create rapport and express appreciation.

It's also crucial to be aware of your actions and surroundings, particularly in residential neighborhoods. Maintain low noise levels, especially late at night, and respect the privacy of local residents. If you're staying in a guesthouse or rental property, familiarize yourself with any house rules and follow them accordingly.

When it comes to photography, always ask for permission before taking pictures of locals or their property. Respecting people's privacy and cultural sensitivity is crucial when visiting Český Krumlov, despite its breathtaking beauty. By obtaining permission before taking images, you will show respect for the community and ensure a positive interaction.

Safety Tips

Although Český Krumlov is generally a safe place, travelers should exercise prudence and common sense to safeguard their well-being throughout their visit. Here are some safety guidelines to bear in mind:

- **Keep a watch on your belongings:** Pickpocketing can happen in popular tourist places, so be cautious and safeguard your valuables. Invest in a money belt or lockable bag to prevent potential thieves, and avoid carrying huge sums of cash or expensive items.

- **Stay hydrated and sun-safe:** If you're exploring Český Krumlov during the summer months, be prepared for hot weather by staying hydrated and wearing sunscreen. Pack a reusable water bottle and use sunscreen on a daily basis to protect your skin from the sun's rays.

- **Stick to designated trails:** If you're planning to hike or explore the surrounding countryside, stick to designated trails and avoid venturing off the beaten path. This not only decreases the likelihood of becoming lost, but it also helps to maintain the natural environment for future generations to enjoy.

- **Be mindful of your surroundings**: Whether you're walking around town or enjoying outdoor activities, be aware of your surroundings and trust your instincts. Avoid dark or abandoned regions at night, and if you're unsure about a situation, take extra precautions and seek help from local authorities or fellow travelers.

- **Have a contingency plan:** While Český Krumlov is a relatively safe destination, it's always wise to have a contingency plan in case of emergencies. Familiarize yourself with the location of the nearest hospital or medical institution, and retain crucial contact information, such as your embassy or consulate, in case you want assistance.

By following these safety tips and staying aware of your surroundings, you can enjoy a worry-free experience in Český Krumlov and focus on creating lasting memories of your time in this enchanting destination.

Environmental Responsibility

As visitors, we have a responsibility to reduce our environmental effect and contribute to the sustainability of the destinations we visit. Český Krumlov, known for its natural beauty and historic charm, emphasizes the importance of environmental stewardship.

Here are ways to lessen your environmental footprint and maintain the beauty of Český Krumlov:

- **Reduce, reuse, and recycle:** Use the three Rs (reduce, reuse, and recycle) to reduce waste and conserve resources during your stay. Carry a reusable water bottle and shopping bag to limit plastic waste, and dispose of trash properly in designated containers.

- **Respect wildlife and ecosystems:** Český Krumlov has various wildlife and habitats, including protected areas around the Vltava River. When exploring nature, step softly and stick to established pathways to prevent disturbing wildlife habitats or harming delicate ecosystems.

- **Choose eco-friendly transportation:** Whenever possible, walk, cycle, or take public transportation. By reducing your carbon footprint, you might gain a new perspective on Český Krumlov and engage with the local population.

- **Support sustainable tourism initiatives:** Look for companies and groups that value sustainability and environmental responsibility. Supporting eco-friendly hotels, local restaurants, and community conservation programs can positively influence Český Krumlov and its citizens.

- **Educate yourself and others:** Learn about the environmental concerns in Český Krumlov and the measures being done to address them. Share your knowledge and experiences with other travelers, and urge them to use sustainable habits on their own journeys.

Making environmentally responsible decisions during your vacation to Český Krumlov can help preserve this unique place for future generations to enjoy. By working together, we can keep Český Krumlov alive and sustainable for future generations.

Chapter 4

ACCOMMODATION OPTIONS

Selecting the right place to stay is pivotal for ensuring a comfortable and memorable experience in Český Krumlov. From quaint guesthouses to opulent hotels, the town offers an array of lodging choices catering to diverse tastes and budgets. This chapter will explore various accommodation options available in Český Krumlov, along with tips for finding the perfect stay.

Hotels

Český Krumlov boasts a selection of hotels ranging from boutique establishments to upscale resorts. These accommodations offer a plethora of amenities, including on-site restaurants, spas, and fitness centers. Many hotels are conveniently located within walking distance of the city center and major attractions, ensuring a convenient and enjoyable stay.

Examples:

- **Hotel Ruze**

Address: Horní 154, 381 01 Český Krumlov, Czechia

Situated in a historic building dating back to the 16th century, Hotel Ruze offers luxurious accommodations with elegant decor and modern amenities. Guests can enjoy fine dining at the hotel's restaurant and relax in the spa and wellness center.

- **Hotel Dvorak Český Krumlov**

Address: Radniční 101, 381 01 Český Krumlov, Czechia

Located on the banks of the Vltava River, Hotel Dvorak offers panoramic views of Český Krumlov Castle. The hotel features comfortable rooms, a rooftop terrace, and an on-site restaurant serving traditional Czech cuisine.

- **Hotel The Old Inn**

Address: Náměstí Svornosti 12, 381 01 Český Krumlov, Czechia

Housed in a historic building dating back to the 16th century, Hotel The Old Inn combines old-world charm with modern comforts. Guests can enjoy spacious rooms, a cozy pub, and a charming courtyard garden.

Guesthouses and Bed & Breakfasts

For travelers seeking a more intimate and personalized experience, guesthouses and bed & breakfasts offer a cozy and welcoming atmosphere. These accommodations are often family-run and provide comfortable rooms and homemade breakfasts, making guests feel right at home.

Examples:

- **Pension Barbakan**

Address: Kaplická 26, 381 01 Český Krumlov, Czechia

Nestled in the heart of Český Krumlov's historic center, Pension Barbakan offers charming rooms with traditional Czech decor. Guests can enjoy a delicious breakfast served in the cozy dining room each morning.

- **Penzion Krumlov**

Address: Linecká 271, 381 01 Český Krumlov, Czechia

Located just a short walk from the city center, Penzion Krumlov offers comfortable accommodations in a peaceful setting. The guesthouse features spacious rooms, a garden terrace, and complimentary bicycle rentals for exploring the area.

- **Penzion Pod Hrazi**

Address: Široká 102, 381 01 Český Krumlov, Czechia

Situated along the banks of the Vltava River, Penzion Pod Hrazi offers picturesque views of Český Krumlov Castle. The guesthouse features cozy rooms, a riverside terrace, and a charming breakfast room serving homemade pastries.

Apartments and Vacation Rentals

For travelers seeking flexibility and independence, apartments and vacation rentals provide an ideal solution. These self-catering accommodations come equipped with kitchens or kitchenettes, allowing guests to prepare their meals and live like locals.

Examples:

- **Apartment U Brány**

Address: Soukenická 54, 381 01 Český Krumlov, Czechia

Located in a historic building just steps from the city center, Apartment U Brány offers spacious accommodations with modern amenities. Guests can enjoy a fully equipped kitchen, a cozy living area, and stunning views of Český Krumlov's rooftops.

- **Apartment Radniční**

Address: Radniční 123, 381 01 Český Krumlov, Czechia

Situated in a quiet residential area, Apartment Radniční offers a peaceful retreat away from the hustle and bustle of the city center. The apartment features a comfortable bedroom, a well-equipped kitchenette, and a private terrace overlooking the surrounding countryside.

- **Vltava Apartments**

Address: Linecká 48, 381 01 Český Krumlov, Czechia

Set in a historic building overlooking the Vltava River, Vltava Apartments offers spacious and stylish accommodations with modern amenities. Guests can enjoy a fully equipped kitchen, a comfortable living area, and panoramic views of Český Krumlov Castle.

Top Recommended Hotels and Resorts

Several hotels and resorts in Český Krumlov frequently receive fantastic reviews, making it easy to choose the ideal accommodation. These hotels provide first-rate amenities, outstanding service, and prime locations, ensuring an unforgettable stay in this gorgeous town. Here are the top recommended hotels and resorts in Český Krumlov:

Hotel Ruze - This ancient hotel is located in a beautifully restored 16th century edifice. Hotel Ruze, situated in the heart of Český Krumlov, has magnificent rooms and suites, a gourmet restaurant, and a spa center with sauna and massage services.

- **Hotel Dvorak Český Krumlov** - Situated on the banks of the Vltava River, Hotel Dvorak offers stunning views of Český Krumlov Castle. The hotel has exquisite rooms, a rooftop patio, and an on-site restaurant that serves traditional Czech cuisine.

- **Hotel The Old Inn** – Hotel The Old Inn, housed in a historic structure on the town center, emanates old-world elegance and sophistication. Guests can enjoy large accommodations, a pleasant tavern, and a lovely courtyard garden.

- **Pension Barbakan** - Nestled in the heart of Český Krumlov's historic center, Pension Barbakan offers cozy accommodations with traditional Czech decor. The hotel is recognized for its friendly staff and delectable handmade breakfasts.

- **Apartment U Brány** - Located just steps from the city center, Apartment U Brány offers spacious and modern accommodations in a historic building. Guests enjoy a fully furnished kitchen, spacious sitting area, and magnificent views of Český Krumlov's rooftops.

Choosing the Right Accommodation for You.

When choosing accommodations in Český Krumlov, take into account your personal tastes, budget, and travel style. Here are some aspects to consider while choosing the perfect lodging for you:

- **Location:** Decide whether you want to stay in the heart of the city center, close to major attractions and restaurants, or prefer a quieter location away from the hustle and bustle.

- **Amenities:** Consider what amenities are important to you, such as free Wi-Fi, parking, breakfast, or on-site facilities like a spa or fitness center.

- **Budget:** Determine your budget for accommodation and look for options that offer good value for money without compromising on quality or comfort.

- **Type of Accommodation:** Choose between hotels, guesthouses, apartments, or vacation rentals based on your preferences for privacy, amenities, and flexibility.

- **Reviews and Ratings:** Read reviews from previous guests to get an idea of the accommodation's quality, cleanliness, and customer service. Look for properties that routinely receive great feedback and high ratings.

Booking Tips and Tricks

Here are some ideas to reserve accommodation in Český Krumlov:

- **Book in Advance:** It is recommended that you book your accommodations well in advance, especially during peak tourist seasons, to assure availability and the best rates.

- **Flexible Dates:** To take advantage of lower rates and more availability, consider traveling during off-peak hours or midweek.

- **Look for Deals:** Keep an eye out for special promotions, discounts, and package deals from hotels and booking platforms.

- **Membership Benefits:** If you're a member of a loyalty program or travel club, check for exclusive discounts or perks when booking accommodation.

- **Contact the property:** If you have any particular requests or requirements, such as food restrictions or accessibility issues, please contact the accommodation directly to discuss your needs and preferences.

Booking Platforms

Online booking systems provide a variety of lodging options in Český Krumlov, making it easier to discover the ideal location to stay. Some popular booking platforms are:

- **Booking.com** - Known for its extensive selection of hotels, guesthouses, and apartments, Booking.com allows you to search and compare accommodations based on price, location, and amenities.

- **Airbnb** - Airbnb offers a variety of unique and personalized accommodation options, including apartments, vacation rentals, and homestays, allowing you to connect with local hosts and experience Český Krumlov like a local.

- **Expedia -** Expedia offers a comprehensive selection of hotels and vacation packages, allowing you to book accommodation, flights, and activities all in one place.

- **Hotels.com** - Hotels.com offers a wide range of accommodation options worldwide, with a Best Price Guarantee and rewards program for frequent travelers.

Using these booking sites and the tips above, you can simply select and book the appropriate hotel for your stay in Český Krumlov. Whether you want elegance, comfort, or affordability, this lovely Czech town has something for everyone.

Český Krumlov offers a variety of lodging alternatives, making it easy to locate the ideal location to stay. Whether you choose a luxurious hotel, a quiet guesthouse, or a roomy apartment, your lodging options will set the tone for an amazing stay in this picturesque Czech town.

Chapter 5

TRANSPORTATION WITHIN ČESKÝ KRUMLOV

Český Krumlov's pedestrian-friendly layout and modest size make it easy to navigate. There are several ways to get around this attractive Czech town and its surrounding landscape, including strolling, cycling, and even taking a scenic boat excursion. This chapter explores transportation options in Český Krumlov and offers helpful advice for efficient travel.

- **Walking.**

Walking is an excellent way to discover Český Krumlov. The town's historic core is very compact and easy to navigate, with most attractions, restaurants, and stores within walking distance of one another. Take your time walking around the cobblestone streets, admiring the medieval architecture, and discovering hidden jewels around every turn.

- **Cycling.**

Cycling is a popular and entertaining way to explore areas outside of the town core. Český Krumlov has various bike rental outlets where you may rent bicycles for a day or more. Cycle along the lovely routes along the Vltava River, explore the surrounding countryside, or take a self-guided bike tour to nearby villages and attractions.

- **Public transportation.**

Although Český Krumlov is fairly accessible, public transit is available for anyone seeking to explore further. The town has a dependable bus station near the city center that provides connections to other towns and villages. Bus services are regular and reasonably priced, making it easy to explore the local area without a car.

- **Taxi**

Taxis are easily accessible in Český Krumlov and can be hailed on the street or reserved in advance. Taxis are a great option for people with luggage or those who need to get to locations outside of the town center fast. Before you begin your journey, clarify the fare with the driver, and always use licensed taxi companies for a safe and trustworthy service.

- **Boat tours**

A picturesque boat cruise along the Vltava River offers a unique way to experience Český Krumlov. Several firms provide guided boat tours that leave from the town center and take visitors on a leisurely journey through the scenic countryside. Relax and enjoy the breathtaking views of Český Krumlov's historic skyline and beautiful greenery from the lake.

Tips for Transportation in Český Krumlov.

- **Plan Ahead:** Choose your mode of transportation based on your itinerary and preferences. Walking is great for exploring the town center, while cycling or taking a boat tour is a unique way to view the surrounding area.
- **Rent a Bike:** Consider renting a bicycle for the duration of your stay to explore Český Krumlov and its beautiful surroundings at your own pace.
- **Use Public Transportation:** Make use of the town's bus terminal for day trips to surrounding sites or villages. Bus services are regular and

reasonably priced, making them an easy method to explore the region.
- **Book Transportation in Advance:** If you want to take a taxi or go on a guided boat tour, reserve ahead of time, especially during peak tourist seasons, to ensure availability.
- **Stay Informed:** To minimize delays or last-minute adjustments, check schedules and routes for public transportation and boat tours in advance.

Exploring Český Krumlov and its surrounding landscape is a beautiful experience, made even more enjoyable by the town's efficient transportation options. Whether you want to stroll, cycle, take public transportation, or take a picturesque boat excursion, you'll make memorable memories as you explore the beauty and charm of this enchanting Czech town.

Chapter 6

DINING AND CULINARY EXPERIENCES

Český Krumlov's unique cuisine is a must-try for any traveler. From traditional Czech meals to cosmopolitan fare, the town's restaurants, cafes, and diners cater to all tastes and preferences. This chapter will walk you through the bustling dining scene in Český Krumlov, highlighting the culinary delights available.

Traditional Czech cuisine:

Explore the traditional foods, flavors, and culinary legacy of Český Krumlov and immerse yourself in the rich tapestry of Czech cuisine. From hearty stews to delicious pastries, each bite tells a tale about history, culture, and custom, enabling visitors to immerse themselves in the true flavors of the Czech Republic. Discover some of the most iconic foods and delicacies of Český Krumlov:

- **Goulash (Guláš):** A beloved Czech classic, goulash is a hearty and comforting stew made with tender beef or pork, onions, peppers, and a rich paprika-infused sauce. Goulash, served sizzling hot with bread or dumplings, is the ultimate comfort food, ideal for warming up on a chilly day.

- **Svíčková:** A popular Czech dish, svíčková is a succulent beef sirloin served with a creamy vegetable sauce made of root vegetables, onions, and sour cream. This flavorful dish is typically served with bread dumplings (houskové knedlíky) and cranberry sauce, resulting in a perfect balance of sweet and savory flavors.

- **Vepřo-knedlo-zelo**: A quintessential Czech dish, vepřo-knedlo-zelo consists of roasted pork served with bread dumplings (knedlíky) and sauerkraut (zelí). The pork is typically seasoned with garlic, caraway seeds, and other aromatic spices before slow roasting to perfection, yielding tender and juicy meat that complements the tangy sauerkraut and hearty dumplings.

- **Trdelník**: A visit to Český Krumlov is incomplete without trying trdelník, a delectable pastry made from rolled dough wrapped around a wooden spindle, grilled until golden brown, and coated in sugar, cinnamon, and chopped nuts. Trdelník is a delicious treat with a crispy exterior and soft interior, satisfying your sweet tooth.

- **Pilsner Beer:** No discussion of Czech cuisine would be complete without mentioning beer, and the Czech Republic is famous for producing some of the world's finest brews. In Český Krumlov, try a pint of Pilsner beer, a light and refreshing lager brewed in Plzeň (Pilsen) since the nineteenth century. Enjoy a cold beer with your meal or on its own, surrounded by good company and lively conversation.

- **Czech Sweets:** Indulge your sweet tooth with a variety of Czech sweets and desserts, including palacinky (thin pancakes) filled with jam or fruit, koláče (fruit-filled pastries), and buchty (sweet buns) stuffed with poppy seeds or plum jam. These delightful treats are ideal for snacking or finishing off a delicious meal with a sweet note.

Where to Find Traditional Czech Cuisine in Český Krumlov?

- **Restaurants:** Explore Český Krumlov's charming restaurants and taverns, where you can sample authentic Czech dishes prepared with care and attention to detail. For an authentic dining experience, seek out restaurants that use locally sourced ingredients and traditional cooking methods.
- **Cafes and Bakeries**: Treat yourself to Czech pastries and desserts at one of Český Krumlov's many cafes and bakeries, where you can indulge in sweet treats like trdelník, koláče, and buchty while soaking in the town's picturesque surroundings.
- **Street Food Stalls:** Keep an eye out for street food stalls and merchants selling Czech specialties during local markets and festivals in Český Krumlov. From grilled sausages and roasted chestnuts to freshly baked pastries and sweet sweets, there's always something delightful to uncover on the streets of Český Krumlov.

Local Specialties:

In the heart of Český Krumlov lies a treasure trove of culinary pleasures, waiting to be found by daring food connoisseurs and curious travelers alike. Delve into the rich tapestry of local delicacies, where each dish offers a narrative of tradition, legacy, and the lively flavors of Czech cuisine. Here's a deeper look into the local delights that await you in Český Krumlov:

- **Česnečka (Garlic Soup):**

Start your gastronomic trip with a bowl of Česnečka, a substantial and soothing garlic soup that is a staple of Czech cuisine. Made with garlic, potatoes, and smoky bacon, Česnečka is commonly served with crispy croutons and fresh parsley, giving texture and taste to this soul-warming dish. It's the perfect way to fight off the chill on a crisp fall day or restore your spirits after a long day of visiting Český Krumlov's cobblestone streets.

- **Trdelník (Chimney Cake):**

Indulge your sweet hunger with a taste of Trdelník, a classic Czech pastry that has become a favorite among locals and visitors alike. Made by wrapping sweet dough around a wooden or metal cylinder, Trdelník is roasted over an open flame until golden brown and crispy on the surface, while soft and doughy on the inside. The final pastry is then covered in sugar and cinnamon, providing a delicious combination of flavors and textures that is sure to satisfy your wants for something sweet.

- **Štrůdl (Strudel):**

A trip to Český Krumlov is not complete without trying the traditional Czech dessert, Štrůdl. Štrůdl, a culinary marvel, is made with thin layers of flaky pastry wrapped around a delightful filling of fruit, nuts, or cheese. It highlights the expertise and workmanship of Czech bakers. Whether you like apple, cherry, or poppy seed filling, each bite of Štrůdl is a symphony of tastes that will take you to gastronomic heaven.

- **Svíčková (Beef Sirloin in Cream Sauce):**

To experience Czech comfort food, try Svíčková, a savory meal with tender beef sirloin marinated in a creamy vegetable sauce. Svíčková, served with dumplings and zesty cranberry sauce, is a beloved classic that will leave you full and content. After a day of sightseeing in Český Krumlov, this meal pairs perfectly with a cold glass of Czech beer or a crisp white wine.

- **Pilsner Urquell:**

Pilsner Urquell, a well-known Czech lager, is a must-try during a visit to Český Krumlov's gastronomic scene. Pilsner Urquell, brewed in adjacent Plzeň (Pilsen) since 1842, is known for its crisp, refreshing taste and golden color, making it the ideal companion to any meal or social occasion. Celebrate Czech brewing tradition and new adventures in Český Krumlov.

Fine Dining Restaurants and Cafés in Český Krumlov

Experience culinary excellence and refined ambiance at Český Krumlov's finest dining establishments. These restaurants and cafés are known for their great cuisine, impeccable service, and attractive settings, providing discerning customers with an unforgettable gourmet experience. Here are some top choices with addresses for easy navigation:

- **Le Jardin.**

Address: Parkán 104, 381 01 Český Krumlov, Czech Republic.

Le Jardin, a historic building overlooking the Vltava River, serves French-inspired food. This Michelin-recommended restaurant has a classy environment and a menu that highlights seasonal and locally produced products. Highlights include pan-seared foie gras, roasted duck breast, and a luscious chocolate soufflé. For a truly unforgettable dining experience, pair your meal with wines from the comprehensive list.

- **Zlatá Koruna**

Address: Panská 96, 381 01 Český Krumlov, Czechia

Step into a bygone era at Zlatá Koruna, nestled in the heart of Český Krumlov's old town. This exquisite restaurant oozes charm and sophistication, serving a menu of refined Czech cuisine made with the best ingredients. Enjoy venison carpaccio, wild boar ragout, and apple strudel with homemade vanilla sauce in an atmosphere evocative of a stately European salon.

- **The Castle Restaurant.**

Address: Zámek 59, 381 01 Český Krumlov, Czechia

Dine like royalty at The Castle Restaurant, situated within the walls of Český Krumlov Castle. This spectacular location provides panoramic views of the town and river below, creating the ideal setting for an outstanding dining experience. Indulge in meals like grilled sea bass, prime ribeye steak, and pear tart with cinnamon ice cream, all cooked with meticulous care and attention to detail.

- **Café Beseda**

Address: Horní 152, 381 01 Český Krumlov, Czechia

Café Beseda is located in the historic town of Český Krumlov and offers a casual yet refined eating experience. This charming café has a warm setting and serves delicious sandwiches, salads, and pastries, as well as a large selection of coffees and teas. Relax on the outdoor terrace and absorb the atmosphere of this traditional European café.

- **Café del Art.**

Address: Latrán 74, 381 01 Český Krumlov, Czechia

Café del Art is a hidden gem among the cobblestone alleyways of Český Krumlov, offering a charming atmosphere. This tiny facility promotes local artwork while also serving delectable pastries, cakes, and light meals, as well as specialty coffees and teas. Sit back, relax, and enjoy the artistic atmosphere while indulging in a sweet treat or savory nibble.

- **Café U Dwau Maryí**

Address: Kájovská 60, 381-01 Český Krumlov, Czechia.

Café U Dwau Maryí offers old-world elegance in a historic edifice from the 16th century. This modest café emanates a warm environment and serves traditional Czech pastries, desserts, and beverages. Enjoy a slice of fresh apple strudel or a cup of creamy hot chocolate while taking in the atmosphere of this charming business.

Tips for Dining in Český Krumlov.

- **Make Reservations:** Reservations are recommended, especially during busy tourist seasons, for fine dining restaurants and popular eateries.
- **Explore Local Markets**: Visit the town's markets and food stalls to try fresh produce, artisanal cheeses, and handcrafted pastries, and meet local sellers and artists.
- **Ask for recommendations:** Ask locals or hotel staff for advice on places to eat. They can provide useful information about hidden treasures and off-the-beaten-path restaurants.
- **Try Something New:** Be adventurous and try new dishes. Český Krumlov's food scene provides numerous flavors and cuisines to discover.
- **Enjoy the experience:** Dining in Český Krumlov is more than simply the food; it's about the overall experience. Take your time savoring each bite, taking in the atmosphere, and making lasting memories with friends and loved ones.

Český Krumlov offers a diverse range of dining options, including traditional Czech cuisine, fine dining, and informal meals. So take a seat, raise your glass, and start on a culinary adventure through this lovely Czech town, where every meal is a celebration of flavor, culture, and friendliness.

Chapter 7

SHOPPING AND ENTERTAINMENT IN ČESKÝ KRUMLOV

Exploring Český Krumlov involves more than simply sightseeing and dining; it's also about experiencing the town's thriving commercial scene and numerous entertainment options. Český Krumlov offers a variety of recreational activities, including shopping, cultural performances, and live music events. This chapter explores retail and leisure choices in Český Krumlov, offering insider advice and ideas for a memorable trip.

Shopping

Local souvenirs and handicrafts:

Exploring the picturesque alleyways of Český Krumlov allows you to not only observe history, but also take a piece of it home. The town's rich cultural legacy is brilliantly captured in its locally manufactured souvenirs and handicrafts, each of which tells a narrative about tradition, workmanship, and Czech identity. Explore Český Krumlov's quaint stores and boutiques to unearth hidden gems. Here's an overview of the local souvenirs and handicrafts available in Český Krumlov:

- **Wooden Toys and Puppets:** One of the most iconic souvenirs of Český Krumlov is its traditional wooden toys and marionettes. These delightful works, made by talented artists employing age-old techniques, ranging from whimsical animals and characters to elaborately detailed puppets based on Czech folklore and fairy tales. Hand-carved wooden toys or puppets from Český Krumlov make great gifts for children or as a unique keepsake for yourself. They will offer delight and nostalgia for years to come.

- **Hand-Painted Ceramics:** Inspired by Český Krumlov's artistic legacy, these hand-painted ceramics add a touch of Bohemian charm to any house. These distinctive items, which range from delicate tea sets and elegant plates to vivid vases and ceramics, highlight the talent and originality of local ceramic craftsmen. Each piece is meticulously created and embellished with elaborate designs and motifs that reflect the town's gorgeous landscapes, historical sites, and folk traditions.

- **Bohemian Crystal Glassware:** For an elegant and timeless souvenir, consider purchasing Bohemian crystal glassware from Český Krumlov. Czech crystal, known for its extraordinary clarity and brilliance, has been sought after for generations. Browse through a collection of exquisitely created glassware, such as sparkling wine glasses, crystal decanters, and elaborately cut bowls, all of which demonstrate the excellent craftsmanship and attention to detail that have made Czech crystal synonymous with elegance and refinement.

- **Handmade Textiles and Embroidery:** Experience Český Krumlov's textile heritage firsthand with a visit to its shops and boutiques specializing in handmade textiles and embroidery. Admire the delicate needlework and brilliant colors of traditional Czech folk costumes, or explore a range of embroidered linens, tablecloths, and pillowcases, all meticulously crafted by expert artists using time-honored traditions passed down through generations. Czech textiles, whether useful or ornamental, are a wonderful and meaningful way to memorialize your vacation to Český Krumlov.

- **Artisanal Food and Beverages:** No visit to Český Krumlov is complete without sampling its delicious artisanal food and beverages. Browse local markets and specialty shops to find a variety of gastronomic treats, such as handcrafted jams and preserves, artisanal cheeses, locally produced honey, and traditional Czech pastries. Take home a bottle of Moravian wine or Czech beer to remember your vacation to Český Krumlov.

Art Galleries and Studios:

Immerse yourself in the vibrant arts scene of Český Krumlov by venturing into its numerous galleries and studios, where creativity flourishes amidst the town's historic backdrop. Český Krumlov's art venues provide a varied selection of works by local and international artists, showcasing the town's rich cultural legacy and creative energy. Explore Český Krumlov's art galleries and studios with insider insights and recommendations for a memorable and fascinating visit.

- **Egon Schiele Art Centrum:**

Address: Široká 71, 381 01 Český Krumlov, Czech Republic

The Egon Schiele Art Centrum, named after the renowned Austrian artist Egon Schiele, is a must-see site for art and cultural fans. The Schiele Center, located in Český Krumlov's Old Town, houses a permanent display of the artist's works, including paintings, sketches, and graphic prints, providing insight into his life and career. In addition to its permanent collection, the center organizes temporary exhibitions of contemporary art by emerging and recognized artists, providing visitors with an engaging and thought-provoking creative experience.

- **Galerie 99:**

Address: Radniční 99, 381 01 Český Krumlov, Czech Republic

Galerie 99, located in the historic city of Český Krumlov, is a lovely art gallery and studio that showcases the works of local artists and crafters. Step inside the gallery to see a broad collection of paintings, sculptures, ceramics, and handmade crafts, each representing the artist's own style and creative vision. Visitors can examine the gallery's collection at their leisure, talk to the artists about their processes and inspirations, and even buy unique items to take home as souvenirs or gifts.

- **Galerie Klatovská 9:**

Address: Klatovská 9, 381 01 Český Krumlov, Czech Republic

Galerie Klatovská 9, located in a historic building within a short walk from the town center, is a hidden gem for art fans and collectors to uncover. The gallery exhibits a wide spectrum of contemporary art by local and international artists, with changing exhibitions of paintings, sculptures, photographs, and mixed-media pieces. In addition to its exhibition space, Galerie Klatovská 9 hosts artist residencies, workshops, and cultural events to promote creativity and collaboration in the local community.

- **Studio of Josef Seidel:**

Address: Latrán 4, 381 01 Český Krumlov, Czech Republic

Visit Josef Seidel's Studio for a one-of-a-kind and immersive art experience. Seidel is a renowned Czech painter and printmaker best recognized for his vivid landscapes and dramatic cityscapes. Located in a historic building overlooking the Vltava River, the studio allows visitors to witness Seidel at work in his creative setting, learn about his artistic process and techniques, and buy original artworks directly from the artist. Whether you're a seasoned art collector or simply admire exquisite craftsmanship, a visit to Josef Seidel's Studio will leave a lasting impact.

Fashion and Jewelry Boutiques:

Indulge your sense of style and adorn yourself with exquisite jewelry by exploring the fashion and jewelry boutiques of Český Krumlov. These shops offer a distinct blend of Czech design, workmanship, and legacy, allowing you to locate the ideal piece to compliment your wardrobe or memorialize your trip to this charming town. Discover the best fashion and jewelry businesses in Český Krumlov, with insider advice for a memorable shopping experience.

- **Boutique name: "Bohemian Chic"**

Address: Latrán 36, 381 01, Český Krumlov, Czech Republic.

Enter Bohemian Chic and immerse yourself in a world of bohemian-inspired clothing and accessories. This boutique features a carefully curated range of apparel, jewelry, and accessories created by local designers and craftspeople. Each piece embodies the rich cultural legacy and artistic energy of Český Krumlov, including flowing maxi skirts, embroidered blouses, striking necklaces, and beaded bracelets. Whether you're looking for a one-of-a-kind keepsake or a trendy addition to your wardrobe, Bohemian Chic has something for every taste and occasion.

- **Boutique name: "Crystal Dreams"**

Address: Radniční 17, 381-01 Český Krumlov, Czech Republic.

Crystal Dreams, a boutique that specializes in handmade crystal jewelry and accessories, invites you to discover the sparkling beauty of Czech crystal. Each piece is painstakingly made by trained artisans utilizing traditional techniques passed down through generations, producing in breathtaking sculptures that shimmer and shine in the light. Crystal Dreams has a large assortment of designs to fit every style and inclination, including delicate earrings and pendants, elaborate brooches, and hair accessories. Whether you're looking for a timeless keepsake or a thoughtful gift, Crystal Dreams has it.

- **Boutique name: "Krumlov Creations"**

Address: Horní 157, 381 01 Český Krumlov, Czech Republic

Krumlov Creations, a store that specializes in handmade fashion and jewelry inspired by Český Krumlov's rich history and culture, offers a unique way to experience the town's beauty. Discover unique apparel, accessories, and jewelry created by local artists and designers in Český Krumlov, showcasing the city's lively arts sector. Whether you're looking for a trendy keepsake or a one-of-a-kind statement piece, Krumlov Creations has a diverse selection of designs to fit every taste or occasion.

Entertainment:

Cultural Performances:

Attend one of Český Krumlov's enthralling cultural performances to learn more about its rich legacy. From classical concerts in ancient locations to traditional folklore performances, these events provide a unique view into the town's rich history, artistic skill, and thriving cultural traditions. Discover the best cultural performances in Český Krumlov, including insider insights and ideas to enhance your visit.

Český Krumlov Castle Theater:

Address: Zámecká 59, 381 01, Český Krumlov, Czech Republic.

The Český Krumlov Castle Theater is one of the world's oldest and best-preserved Baroque theaters, transporting visitors back in time. This historic theater, which dates back to the 17th century, has been painstakingly restored to its former magnificence and now hosts a range of cultural activities throughout the year, including opera, ballet, drama, and classical music concerts. Set against the castle's stately halls, these performances transport spectators to a bygone era of elegance and refinement, providing an unparalleled cultural experience.

Tips:

- **Book Tickets in Advance:** Due to the popularity of performances at the Český Krumlov Castle Theater, it's advisable to book tickets in advance to secure your seats, especially during peak tourist seasons.
- **Arrive Early:** Arrive early to explore the castle grounds and take in the breathtaking views of Český Krumlov from the castle's terraces before the performance begins.

- **Dress Code:** While there is no strict dress code for castle theater performances, wearing carefully will match the exquisite location and improve your overall experience.

Czech folklore performances:

Address: Various locations in Český Krumlov

Experience Czech culture through vibrant folklore performances in Český Krumlov. These engaging concerts comprise traditional music, dancing, and theatrical reenactments of age-old customs and ceremonies, shedding light on the country's rural heritage and folk traditions. From lively polka dances to lyrical folk tunes, these performances highlight the Czech Republic's vivid spirit and cultural diversity, providing an authentic and immersive experience for audiences of all ages.

Tips:

- **Check Local Listings:** Keep an eye on local event listings and tourist information centers for upcoming folklore performances in Český Krumlov.
- **Attend Festivals:** Many folklore performances take place during festivals and special events

throughout the year, allowing tourists to experience Czech culture in a festive and celebratory setting.
- **Engage with the Performers:** Do not be scared to interact with the performers and learn more about the traditions and rituals depicted in the show. Many performers are eager to offer stories and insights into their cultural history with interested audiences.

Outdoor concerts and events:

Address: Various outdoor venues in Český Krumlov.

Outdoor concerts and festivals in Český Krumlov offer opportunities to enjoy music and community. Throughout the summer, the town comes alive with a variety of outdoor entertainment, including as concerts, street acts, and cultural festivals. Outdoor events in Český Krumlov provide a joyous and inclusive atmosphere for people and visitors to celebrate the arts and enjoy the beauty of the town's outdoor areas, ranging from classical music beneath the stars to colorful street performers in the town center.

Tips:

- **Pack a Picnic:** Bring a blanket, snacks, and drinks to enjoy a picnic while you soak in the sounds of live music in Český Krumlov's picturesque outdoor venues.
- **Check Event Calendars**: Check event calendars and local listings for upcoming outdoor concerts and events in Český Krumlov.
- **Arrive Early:** Arrive early to get a good seat and enjoy the pre-concert activities and entertainment before the main performance begins.

Cultural performances in Český Krumlov provide a unique opportunity to experience the town's rich cultural heritage and artistic traditions. Experience unforgettable performances in Český Krumlov, including the Baroque beauty of the castle theater, Czech folk music, and outdoor concerts under the stars.

Live Music and Nightlife:

As the sun sets over the picturesque town of Český Krumlov, a vibrant nightlife scene comes to life, offering travelers a diverse array of options for evening entertainment. Český Krumlov's nightlife offers a variety of options, including comfortable pubs, vibrant bars, and intimate live music venues. Visitors may unwind and interact after a day of exploring. A comprehensive guide to Český Krumlov's live music and nightlife, with insider insights and ideas for an amazing evening.

1. COZY PUBS AND BARS:

- **Eggenberg Brewery**

Address: Latrán 27, 381 01 Český Krumlov, Czechia

Visit Eggenberg Brewery, one of the Czech Republic's oldest breweries, to learn about the brewing history of Český Krumlov. Eggenberg Brewery, housed in a historic building near the town center, provides a comfortable and inviting ambiance in which to enjoy a selection of traditional Czech beers brewed on-site. Choose from classic lagers, ales, and specialty brews, and match them with substantial pub grub for a filling evening of food and drinks.

- **Club Shadow**

Address: Panská 19, 381 01 Český Krumlov, Czechia

Club Shadow, located in the historic town of Český Krumlov, offers a dynamic and energetic nightlife experience. Dance the night away to the newest songs and classics spun by resident DJs, or drink freshly prepared cocktails while socializing with locals and fellow tourists. Club Shadow's colorful environment and late-night hours make it the ideal spot for anyone wishing to unwind and have a great time.

2. INTIMATE LIVE MUSIC VENUES:

- **Jazz Club Apollon**

Address: Radniční 29, 381 01 Český Krumlov, Czechia

Jazz Club Apollon, located in the historic town of Český Krumlov, offers a comfortable and intimate atmosphere for jazz lovers. Enjoy live performances by local and worldwide jazz musicians in a casual and welcoming atmosphere where the music takes center stage. Enjoy great wines, drinks, and spirits while listening to the heartfelt songs and improvisations of some of the region's most gifted musicians.

- **Klub Mír.**

Address: Parkán 105, 381 01 Český Krumlov, Czechia

Klub Mír, a vibrant venue in Český Krumlov, offers a diverse range of live music events, including rock, blues, folk, and electronic music. Klub Mír, located in a historic building overlooking the Vltava River, provides an intimate and laid-back ambiance for enjoying concerts by local bands and musicians while sipping cold beers and beverages.

Outdoor Activities and Events:

- **Rafting and Canoeing on the Vltava River:**

Experience the thrill of rafting or canoeing along the scenic Vltava River in Český Krumlov. Join a guided tour or hire a canoe or raft from a local outfitter and enjoy a leisurely paddle downstream, taking in the breathtaking vistas of the surrounding hills, forests, and historic landmarks along the way. Whether you're an experienced paddler or a first-time explorer, exploring the Vltava River by boat guarantees a memorable experience full of thrills and natural beauty.

- **Guided Walking and Hiking Tours:**

Experience the hidden gems of Český Krumlov and its surrounding countryside with a guided walking or hiking tour conducted by skilled local guides. Choose from a selection of themed tours, such as historical walks through the town's medieval alleyways, nature treks along scenic trails, and culinary trips that showcase the region's traditional cuisine and heritage. Discover Český Krumlov's rich history, cultural traditions, and natural attractions while exploring its quaint alleys, verdant forests, and rolling hillsides with professional guides who are passionate about sharing their love for the town with people from across the world.

- **Cycling and Mountain Biking Adventures:**

Explore Český Krumlov's gorgeous countryside on a cycling or mountain riding journey for a fresh perspective of the town and its surroundings. Rent a bike from a local store and embark on a self-guided tour of the area's scenic bike lanes, or join a guided cycling adventure that takes you off the beaten road to discover hidden jewels and stunning views. Whether you're a casual cyclist or a seasoned mountain biker, Český Krumlov's diverse terrain and stunning landscape provide the perfect backdrop for an amazing two-wheeled trip.

- **Outdoor Events and Festivals:**

Český Krumlov celebrates its cultural legacy, artistic creativity, and natural beauty through outdoor events and festivals all year round. Český Krumlov has a variety of entertaining activities for guests of all ages, including music and arts festivals, gastronomic events, and historical reenactments. Check the town's event calendar for upcoming outdoor events and festivals during your visit. Participate in the celebrations and experience Český Krumlov's vibrant community spirit firsthand.

Insider Tips for Shopping and Entertainment:

- **Explore Off the Beaten Path:** Go beyond the typical tourist destinations to find hidden gems and locally owned stores and galleries.
- **Shop Local:** Help the town's craftsmen and small businesses by purchasing locally manufactured products and souvenirs.
- **Check Event Calendars:** Keep a look out for forthcoming concerts, exhibitions, and festivals during your visit.
- **Plan Ahead for Popular Attractions:** If you want to attend a specific performance or event, consider reserving tickets ahead of time to ensure your spot.

- Be open to new experiences and explore the diverse retail and entertainment options in Český Krumlov. You never know what treasures you could discover or memories you might make along the road.

Český Krumlov's shopping and entertainment options combine culture, innovation, and excitement, allowing visitors to thoroughly immerse themselves in the town's beauty and warmth. Český Krumlov offers amazing experiences, such as shopping local shops for handmade treasures, attending cultural performances at the castle, or dancing the night away at a live music venue, leaving you wanting to return again and again.

Chapter 8

ITINERARIES FOR DIFFERENT TRAVELERS

So, you're planning your adventure in Český Krumlov, and you want to make the most of your time here, right? Well, you've come to the right place! In this chapter, I'll walk you through a variety of itineraries tailored to different types of travelers. Whether you're here for just a day or you have a few days to spare, I've got you covered with some fantastic suggestions to ensure you have an unforgettable experience.

Weekend Getaway

Day 1

Morning:

Begin your day with a visit to Český Krumlov Castle. Explore its grand halls and magnificent gardens while learning about its rich history. Don't forget to climb the castle tower for breathtaking views of the city.

Afternoon:

Head to the historic city center for a leisurely lunch at one of the charming local restaurants. Afterward, take a stroll along the cobblestone streets, admiring the colorful buildings and stopping in at the Egon Schiele Art Centrum.

Evening:

Enjoy dinner at a cozy restaurant with traditional Czech cuisine. Then, take a twilight walk along the Vltava River, soaking in the magical atmosphere of Český Krumlov at night.

Day 2

Morning:

Start your day with a scenic hike or bike ride in the surrounding countryside. Explore the picturesque landscapes and enjoy the fresh air and tranquility.

Afternoon:

Visit the Český Krumlov Regional Museum to delve deeper into the area's culture and heritage. Afterwards, indulge in a delicious lunch at a local tavern.

Evening:

Savor a romantic dinner at a riverside restaurant, followed by a moonlit stroll through the illuminated streets of the city center.

Cultural Immersion

Day 1

Morning:

Embark on a guided tour of Český Krumlov Castle, immersing yourself in centuries of history and architecture. Discover the stories behind the castle's walls and marvel at its intricate details.

Afternoon:

Delve into the heart of Český Krumlov's cultural scene with a visit to the Baroque Theater. Experience the magic of a live performance or take a backstage tour to learn about its fascinating history.

Evening:

Satisfy your appetite with a traditional Czech dinner at a local tavern, accompanied by live folk music and dancing.

Day 2

Morning:

Explore the winding streets of the city center, taking in its architectural treasures and hidden gems. Visit St. Vitus Church and admire its stunning interior before continuing your journey.

Afternoon:

Indulge in a leisurely lunch at a cozy cafe, sampling local delicacies and sipping on Czech beer or wine.

Afterwards, peruse the artisanal shops and galleries, where you can find unique souvenirs and gifts.

Evening:

Attend a cultural event or performance, such as a classical concert or traditional folk dance performance, to cap off your immersive experience in Český Krumlov.

Adventure Seekers Itinerary

Day 1

Morning:

Kickstart your adrenaline-filled weekend with an exhilarating whitewater rafting or kayaking adventure on the Vltava River. Navigate through rapids and enjoy the stunning scenery along the way.

Afternoon:

Refuel with a hearty lunch at a riverside restaurant, then gear up for an afternoon of outdoor activities. Choose from options like rock climbing, zip-lining, or mountain biking, all within easy reach of Český Krumlov.

Evening:

Relax and unwind after your action-packed day with a barbecue dinner and bonfire under the stars. Share stories of your adventures with fellow travelers and soak in the natural beauty of your surroundings.

Day 2

Morning:

Embark on a thrilling canopy walk through the treetops of the Bohemian Forest, taking in panoramic views of the landscape below. Keep an eye out for local wildlife as you navigate the suspended bridges and platforms.

Afternoon:

Challenge yourself with a high ropes course or aerial adventure park experience, testing your balance and agility amidst the forest canopy.

Evening:

Celebrate your adventurous weekend with a farewell dinner at a local restaurant, sharing memories and laughs with your fellow thrill-seekers.

Family-Friendly Itinerary

Day 1

Morning:

Start your family getaway with a visit to Český Krumlov Castle, where kids can embark on a fun-filled treasure hunt or explore the castle's interactive exhibits.

Afternoon:

Enjoy a picnic lunch in the castle gardens, then take a leisurely stroll through the city center, stopping to admire the whimsical Marionette Museum and browse the toy shops.

Evening:

Treat the whole family to a traditional Czech dinner at a family-friendly restaurant, followed by a relaxing evening stroll along the river.

Day 2

Morning:

Spend the morning exploring the Bear Sanctuary, where kids can learn about conservation efforts and observe rescued bears in their natural habitat.

Afternoon:

Take a scenic bike ride along the Vltava River, stopping at playgrounds and parks along the way for some outdoor fun.

Evening:

End your family adventure with a special dinner cruise on the river, complete with onboard entertainment and stunning sunset views.

Budget Travel

Day 1

Morning:

Start your budget-friendly getaway with a self-guided tour of Český Krumlov Castle, taking advantage of discounted admission rates during off-peak hours.

Afternoon:

Opt for a picnic lunch in one of the city's scenic parks or green spaces, where you can enjoy delicious local snacks without breaking the bank.

Evening:

Explore the city's free attractions, such as the historic city center and St. Vitus Church, before indulging in an affordable dinner at a local tavern or street food vendor.

Day 2

Morning:

Take advantage of free walking tours or cultural events offered by local organizations, where you can learn about Český Krumlov's history and culture from knowledgeable guides.

Afternoon:

Explore the city's public art installations and street performances, or visit the Český Krumlov Regional Museum, which offers discounted admission on certain days of the week.

Evening:

Wrap up your budget-friendly adventure with a picnic dinner by the river, watching the sunset over Český Krumlov's picturesque skyline.

Romantic Getaway Itinerary

Day 1

Morning:

Start your romantic getaway with a private tour of Český Krumlov Castle, where you can wander hand in hand through its enchanting gardens and hidden courtyards.

Afternoon:

Indulge in a leisurely lunch at a quaint cafe in the city center, then spend the afternoon exploring the charming streets and boutique shops, stopping to admire the works of local artisans.

Evening:

Dine in style at a romantic restaurant with a view, where you can enjoy candlelit dinners and fine Czech wines as you toast to your love.

Day 2

Morning:

Take a scenic hot air balloon ride over the city and countryside, enjoying panoramic views of Český Krumlov from above.

Afternoon:

Relax and unwind with a couples' spa day, indulging in massages, hot tubs, and other luxurious treatments.

Evening:

End your romantic getaway with a moonlit walk along the river, followed by a private dinner cruise under the stars. Snuggle up together as you drift along the tranquil waters, savoring the magic of Český Krumlov at night.

No matter which itinerary you choose, Český Krumlov promises to enchant and captivate you with its beauty, history, and charm. So pack your bags, embark on your journey, and prepare to create memories that will last a lifetime in this magical Czech gem.

Chapter 9

EVENTS AND FESTIVALS

Every year, Český Krumlov hosts a variety of festivals and events that showcase the town's rich cultural heritage and vibrant personality. Český Krumlov hosts a variety of interesting events, including music and arts performances, historical reenactments, and culinary feasts, inviting tourists to join in the fun. In this chapter, we'll highlight some of the most cherished festivals and events in Český Krumlov, providing necessary insights and dates for an amazing experience.

- **Český Krumlov International Music Festival:**

Date: Late June to early July

The Český Krumlov International Music Festival showcases a harmonic convergence of classical music. This two-week spectacle, held yearly from late June to early July, features spectacular performances by world-class artists, orchestras, and ensembles in the town's historic sites. From tiny chamber concerts to enormous orchestral spectacles, the festival takes listeners on a captivating voyage through the worlds of classical music, enriching the soul and stimulating the senses.

- **Five-Petalled Rose Celebrations:**

Date: mid-June.

Step back in time to the medieval past at the exquisite Five-Petalled Rose Celebrations, which take place in mid-June. The immersive festival transforms Český Krumlov's historic center into a lively medieval marketplace, complete with costumed entertainers, crafters, and jesters. Enjoy the pomp of the grand procession, traditional games and activities, and period-inspired feasts fit for royalty. The Five-Petalled Rose Celebrations provide a unique opportunity to explore Český Krumlov's medieval heritage.

- **Český Krumlov Castle Celebrations:**

Date: Various dates throughout the year

The Český Krumlov Castle Celebrations take place on various dates throughout the year, offering a glimpse into history. These varied events honor the castle's storied history with a potpourri of historical reenactments, dramatic performances, and immersive experiences. Explore Český Krumlov's castle, gardens, and cultural heritage. Whether you're fascinated by medieval legends or Baroque magnificence, the Castle Celebrations guarantee an exciting journey through time.

- **Czech Beer Festival:**

Date: late August

Raise a drink to Czech beer culture during the colorful Czech Beer Festival, which takes place in late August. This festive festival in Český Krumlov's town square features a variety of locally brewed beverages from Czech breweries. Enjoy the different flavors of classic lagers, ales, and pilsners, accompanied by live music, excellent Czech cuisine, and lively conversation. Whether you're a seasoned beer enthusiast or a casual drinker, the Czech Beer Festival is a must-see event for anyone who enjoys good times and great beer.

Insider tips for festivals and events:

- **Plan Ahead**: Consult the event calendar and schedule your visit to coincide with festivals and events that interest you. Book your lodgings and

tickets well in advance, especially during high seasons.
- **Arrive Early:** Arrive early to festivals and events to secure good viewing positions and avoid long lines. Consider purchasing tickets online to speed up the admittance process.
- **Dress Appropriately:** Dress comfortably and appropriately for outdoor events, taking into account weather conditions and venue specifications. Layering is recommended for changing temperatures or bad weather.
- **Sample local delicacies:** Enjoy the culinary delights presented at festivals and events, including traditional Czech cuisine and regional delicacies. Accept the opportunity to satisfy your taste senses with authentic flavors and culinary delights.
- **Respect Local Customs:** Celebrate the essence of each celebration and event while respecting local customs and traditions. Follow event standards and restrictions to establish an environment of mutual respect and cultural understanding.

Festivals and events in Český Krumlov capture the town's vivid personality and cultural vigor, inviting visitors to join in the fun and create lasting memories. Whether you enjoy classical music, medieval pageantry, or Czech beer, Český Krumlov's festivals and events provide an immersive trip into the heart and soul of this charming town.

Chapter 10

PRACTICAL TIPS

To have a memorable trip to Český Krumlov, it's important to have practical information and insights beforehand. These practical suggestions will help you navigate Český Krumlov's cobblestone streets and enjoy its culinary pleasures while avoiding usual mistakes and problems. Let's get started with some basic tips to help you make the most of your visit to this attractive Czech town.

Packing essentials:

- Comfortable footwear (such as robust walking shoes or mountaineering boots)
- Weather-appropriate Clothing (e.g., lightweight and breathable clothing for summer, layers for spring and autumn, and warm layers for winter)
- Daypack or Bag (e.g., lightweight, durable bag with several pockets)
- Travel accessories (such as a travel adaptor, portable charger, and travel pillow)

- Personal Items (e.g., toiletries, medications, sunscreen, hat, sunglasses)
- Travel documents (such as a passport, travel insurance, itinerary, and maps)
- Camera or Smartphone (to capture memories)
- Snacks and water bottle (to keep you hydrated and energized while exploring)
- Rain gear or umbrella (to shield from rain showers)
- Guidebook or Language Translator (to navigate the town and communicate with people).

Currency and payment:

Knowing the currency and payment methods in Český Krumlov is crucial for a smooth travel experience in the Czech Republic. From getting cash to completing transactions at local places, understanding the currency system and payment choices ensures that your financial interactions run well during your visit. Explore the practical aspects of money exchange, ATMs, and payment etiquette in Český Krumlov.

Czech Koruna (CZK):

The Czech Republic's official currency is the Czech Koruna (CZK), abbreviated as Kč. While some companies accept euros or major credit cards, it's best to keep Czech Koruna on hand for everyday purchases, particularly at smaller places, markets, and taxis. Familiarize yourself with the denominations and exchange rates to minimize confusion when handling money.

Accessing Cash:

ATMs are readily available in Český Krumlov, especially in the town center and near important attractions. Look for ATMs operated by major banks, which frequently provide instructions in various languages and accept foreign debit and credit cards. Be aware of ATM fees and currency conversion charges, which may differ depending on your card issuer.

Currency exchange offices, or "směnárna" in Czech, are common throughout Český Krumlov's tourist attractions, such as the town square and main streets. Before exchanging currency, compare exchange rates and fees, and consider exchanging only what you need to avoid incurring additional expenses or having spare currency.

Payment methods:

- **Cash:** Cash is widely accepted in Český Krumlov, particularly for small purchases, street vendors, and local markets. Carry enough Czech Koruna to cover everyday expenses including food, souvenirs, and transportation costs.
- **Credit and Debit Cards:** Major credit cards, such as Visa and Mastercard, are accepted at most hotels, restaurants, and shops in Český Krumlov, especially in tourist areas. However, smaller shops and rural regions may prefer cash payments or take just a limited number of cards, so keep cash on hand as a backup.
- **Contactless Payments:** Contactless payment methods, such as mobile wallets and contactless cards, are becoming increasingly popular in Český Krumlov, especially in urban areas and modern establishments. Before you use contactless payments, check with your card issuer to ensure compatibility and security features.

Currency Exchange Tip:

- **Exchange Rates:** Compare exchange rates and fees at multiple currency exchange offices to get the best value for your money. Avoid exchanging

currency at airports or tourist destinations, where exchange rates may be lower.
- **Currency Conversion:** Be wary of dynamic currency conversion (DCC) offers at ATMs and POS terminals, which allow you to pay in your native currency but sometimes result in greater fees and unfavorable exchange rates. To avoid unnecessary charges, pay in local currency (Czech Koruna).
- **Receipt and documentation:** Keep receipts and transaction records for currency swaps and ATM withdrawals, particularly when converting significant quantities of money or using foreign cards, for future reference and possible reimbursement in the event of inconsistencies or disputes.

Payment Etiquette:

- **Tipping:** Tipping is customary in Český Krumlov, with gratuities typically ranging from 10% to 15% of the total bill in restaurants and cafes. Before tipping, check the bill to see whether there is a service charge, then either hand cash to the server or leave it on the table.
- **Split Payments:** When dining in groups, especially at restaurants and cafés, inquire about split payments or separate checks to ensure

smooth payment arrangements and to minimize confusion.
- **Card Transactions:** When making a payment by card, wait for the transaction to be processed and authorized before removing your card or signing the receipt. To avoid unwanted access, keep your PIN hidden and protected during card transactions.

Navigating money and payments in Český Krumlov takes planning, alertness, and adaptability to enable smooth and efficient transactions. To confidently handle your finances in Český Krumlov, it's important to learn the local currency, access cash through ATMs or currency exchange offices, and grasp payment methods and etiquette.

Language and Communication:

Although English is widely spoken in Český Krumlov, learning the local language and communication nuances can enhance your vacation experience and establish important interactions with the locals. Here are some deep insights and practical recommendations to help you along your linguistic journey:

Embracing Czech Phrases:

While basic English is understood in most tourist places, learning a few Czech words can show respect for the local culture and improve your relationships with the locals. Here are some key phrases to add to your repertoire:

- **Dobrý den (dob-ree den):** "Good day" or "Hello." Use this polite greeting when entering shops, restaurants, or engaging with locals.
- **Prosim (pro-seem):** "Please." Employ this word when making requests or seeking assistance.
- **Děkuji (dyeh-koo-yee):** "Thank you." Express gratitude with this simple phrase, acknowledging acts of kindness or hospitality.
- **Ano (ah-no):** "Yes" and Ne (neh): "No." Mastering these affirmative and negative responses can facilitate smoother interactions in various contexts.

Practicing these phrases not only enhances communication but also fosters a sense of cultural appreciation and goodwill during your Český Krumlov adventure.

Language-learning resources:

There are several tools available to help tourists improve their language skills before and during their journey.

- **Language Apps:** Download language-learning apps such as Duolingo, Babbel, or Rosetta Stone to familiarize yourself with Czech vocabulary, pronunciation, and grammar. These interactive platforms provide lessons geared toward various competency levels, allowing you to learn at your own speed.
- **Phrasebooks and Guides**: Purchase a Czech phrasebook or language guide to keep with you during your travels. These pocket-sized materials provide instant access to key phrases and expressions, preparing you for impromptu conversations and interactions.
- **Language Classes**: Consider enrolling in a local language class or workshop upon arrival in Český Krumlov. Many language schools and cultural institutes provide intensive courses created specifically for tourists, allowing them to learn conversational Czech in a supportive setting.

By immersing yourself in the Czech language using these tools, you will not only improve your trip experience but will also form stronger bonds with the local culture and community.

Cross-cultural Communication Tips:

Managing cross-cultural communication takes sensitivity, understanding, and an open mind. Here are some more strategies to enhance meaningful interactions with locals:

- **Nonverbal Communication:** Facial expressions, gestures, and body language can all convey meaning and feelings in Czech culture.
- **Active Listening:** Practice active listening by giving your full attention to speakers, maintaining eye contact, and nodding or providing verbal cues to show understanding.
- **Cultural Sensitivity:** Follow cultural norms and conventions, such as approaching seniors with respect and refraining from intrusive questions or topics of conversation.
- **Patience and Perseverance:** Approach language barriers with patience and perseverance, embracing mistakes as opportunities for learning and growth. Locals value real attempts to communicate, even if language skills are poor.

To enrich your experience in Český Krumlov, practice cross-cultural communication skills, study Czech phrases, and use language-learning tools. Language becomes a bridge that crosses countries, building ties that last long after your travels are over.

WiFi and Connectivity:

In today's digital age, being connected when traveling is more crucial than ever, allowing you to obtain directions, communicate with loved ones, and share your experiences with the rest of the world. Český Krumlov offers Wi-Fi and connectivity solutions to stay connected during your travel. Here's an in-depth look of Wi-Fi and connectivity in Český Krumlov, with helpful recommendations for staying connected.

Wi-Fi availability:

- **Accommodations:** Many hotels, guesthouses, and hostels in Český Krumlov offer complimentary Wi-Fi access for guests. Before reserving your accommodation, check to see if

Wi-Fi is included and inquire about the connection's quality and reliability.
- **Restaurants and Cafes:** Numerous restaurants, cafes, and eateries in Český Krumlov provide free Wi-Fi for patrons. Whether you're having a leisurely lunch or grabbing a quick coffee, you can usually find Wi-Fi to check emails, browse the internet, or post photos of your culinary pleasures.
- **Tourist Information Centers:** The tourist information centers in Český Krumlov may offer free Wi-Fi access for visitors. Visit one of these locations to obtain maps, brochures, and other travel information while remaining connected online.

Mobile Data and SIM Card:

- **Local SIM Cards:** For tourists who demand constant connectivity, getting a local SIM card is a practical solution. Purchase a SIM card and data plan from a mobile network provider's store in Český Krumlov. This option allows you to use mobile data to browse the internet, navigate, and communicate while visiting the town.
- **Portable Wi-Fi Devices:** Another alternative for visitors looking for reliable internet access on the fly is to rent a portable Wi-Fi device. Pocket Wi-Fi

devices, also known as mobile hotspots, provide internet connectivity for several devices simultaneously, allowing you to stay connected anywhere in Český Krumlov and beyond.

Connectivity Tips:

- **Check Coverage Areas:** While Český Krumlov is relatively well-connected, rural areas or outdoor locations may have limited or no Wi-Fi or mobile data coverage. Plan your activities accordingly and save offline maps or instructions for regions with weak connectivity.
- **Wi-Fi Security:** When using public Wi-Fi networks, take care to protect your personal information and sensitive data. Avoid logging into sensitive accounts or doing financial transactions on insecure networks, and consider utilizing a virtual private network (VPN) for enhanced security.
- **Roaming Charges:** If you intend to utilize your mobile phone's data roaming feature, be aware of any potential roaming charges from your home network operator. To minimize surprise penalties, consider purchasing an overseas roaming package or data plan.

Stay connected while experiencing Český Krumlov's historic buildings, quaint streets, and picturesque scenery using available Wi-Fi and connectivity choices. These ideas can help you make the most of your trip to Český Krumlov, whether you're sharing updates with friends and family, using internet maps, or remaining connected for peace of mind.

Sustainable Travel Practices:

- **Reduce Waste**: Bring a reusable water bottle and shopping bag to minimize plastic waste and support eco-friendly initiatives in Český Krumlov.
- **Respect the Environment:** When engaging in outdoor activities, follow the Leave No Trace principles by disposing of garbage respectfully and respecting natural habitat.

Health & Wellness:

- **Travel Insurance:** Consider purchasing travel insurance to cover medical emergencies, trip cancellations, and other unforeseen circumstances during your visit to Český Krumlov.

- **Health Services:** Familiarize yourself with the location of medical facilities, pharmacies, and emergency services in Český Krumlov in case of medical assistance.

Incorporating these practical ideas into your trip planning will help you explore Český Krumlov confidently and easily, allowing you to enjoy the town's beauty, culture, and warmth. Make the most of your Český Krumlov vacation by discovering historic landmarks, experiencing local cuisine, and immersing yourself in cultural experiences. These insights will help you create lasting memories to treasure for years to come.

CONCLUSION

So there you have it – your complete guide to exploring the enchanting town of Český Krumlov! This hidden jewel in the Czech Republic, with its medieval splendor and dynamic cultural scene, has something for everyone.

Let me recap our tour and conclude with some final suggestions and recommendations to guarantee your stay is nothing short of memorable.

Final Tips and Recommendations

Before leaving Český Krumlov, consider these final advices for a smooth and joyful departure:

- Take some time to explore the town's artisan shops and galleries, where you'll find unique souvenirs and gifts to remind you of your time in Český Krumlov.
- Consider purchasing a Český Krumlov Card, which offers discounts on admission to many of the town's top attractions and activities.

- Enjoy the delights of Czech food during your stay, from substantial goulash to sweet dumplings. Be sure to try a traditional Czech beer or two, produced with care using centuries-old recipes.
- Finally, pause and enjoy the beauty and peacefulness of Český Krumlov's medieval streets and historic landmarks. Whether you're watching the sunset from the castle tower or simply strolling down the cobblestone alleyways, treasure the memories you've built in this magical town.

As you leave Český Krumlov, remember that you will carry the spirit of this timeless location with you, not just images and souvenirs. It will stay with you long after you return home.

Safe travels, and until we meet again, na shledanou!

APPENDIX: USEFUL RESOURCES

Emergency Contacts

In case of any emergencies during your visit to Český Krumlov, it's essential to have access to local emergency contacts:

- Police: 158
- Ambulance: 155
- Fire Department: 150
- Medical Emergency: 112
- Tourist Police: +420 974 822 909
- Český Krumlov Hospital: +420 380 731 111
- Poison Control Center: +420 224 919 293
- Non-Emergency Police (Local Station): +420 380 704 311
- Tourist Information Center (for general assistance): +420 380 704 622
- Český Krumlov Municipal Office (for administrative inquiries): +420 380 755 111
- Veterinary Emergency Services: +420 773 700 303

- Roadside Assistance: +420 1230 (for breakdowns and vehicle assistance)
- Lost and Found Office (for lost items): +420 380 704 634

Save these numbers in your phone or write them down in a convenient location for quick reference.

Maps and Navigational Tools

Navigating the winding streets and historic landmarks of Český Krumlov is made easier with the help of maps and navigational tools:

- **Offline Maps:** Download offline maps of Český Krumlov using apps such as Google Maps or Maps.me to access them even without internet connection.
- **Tourist Information Center:** Visit the Tourist Information Center in Český Krumlov to pick up free maps and brochures, or ask for assistance with navigation and directions. https://www.visitceskykrumlov.cz/en/services-cesky-krumlov/tourist-information-centre-cesky-krumlov/12-154/

- **Google Maps:** Google Maps: https://www.google.com/maps
- **Mapy.cz:** A popular Czech map application with hiking and biking route options https://en.mapy.cz/

Additional Reading and References

Deepen your understanding of Český Krumlov's history, culture, and attractions with these additional reading and reference materials:

- **Lonely Planet Czech Republic**: Lonely Planet Czech Republic: https://www.lonelyplanet.com/czech-republic
- **Rick Steves Czech Republic:** Rick Steves Czech Republic: [invalid URL removed]
- **The Official Website of Český Krumlov:** https://www.ckrumlov.cz/cz/mesto-cesky-krumlov/

Useful Local Phrases

While English is widely spoken in Český Krumlov, knowing a few basic Czech phrases can enhance your travel experience and help you connect with locals:

Basic Greetings and Politeness:

- Dobré ráno (DOH-breh RAH-noh) - Good morning
- Dobrý večer (DOH-bree VEH-cher) - Good evening
- Dobrou noc (DOH-broh nohts) - Good night
- Prosím (PRO-seem) - Please
- Děkuji (DYEH-koo-yee) - Thank you
- Prosím vás (PRO-seem vahs) - Excuse me/sorry
- Promiňte (pro-MEEN-teh) - Pardon me

Asking for Information:

- Mluvíte anglicky? (MLOO-vee-teh ahn-GLEETS-kee) - Do you speak English?
- Můžete mi pomoci? (MOO-zheh-teh mee POH-moh-tsee) - Can you help me?
- Kde je...? (kdeh yeh) - Where is...?

- Kolik to stojí? (KO-lik toh STO-yee) - How much does it cost?

Ordering Food and Drinks:

- Jeden pivo, prosím. (YE-den PEE-voh, PRO-seem) - One beer, please.
- Jídelní lístek, prosím. (YEE-dehl-nee LEES-tek, PRO-seem) - Menu, please.
- Mám alergii na... (mahm ah-LEHR-ghee nah) - I have an allergy to...
- Dobrou chuť! (DOH-broh khookht) - Bon appétit!

Making Small Talk:

- Jak se máte? (yahk seh MAH-teh) - How are you? (formal)
- Jak se máš? (yahk seh MAHSH) - How are you? (informal)
- Co děláte dnes? (tsoh DEH-la-teh dnes) - What are you doing today?
- Líbí se mi Český Krumlov. (LEE-bee seh mee CHESS-kee KROOM-lohv) - I like Český Krumlov.

Emergency Situations:

- Pomoc! (POH-mots) - Help!

- Potřebuji lékaře. (po-TZHE-booh-yee LEH-kah-ryeh) - I need a doctor.
- Zavolejte policii! (za-vo-LEY-teh poh-lee-TSEE) - Call the police!
- Hasiči jsou potřeba! (hasi-tchi ysoh pot-zhe-ba) - Firefighters are needed!

Shopping and Negotiating:

- Můžu to vidět? (MOO-zhoo toh VIH-deht) - Can I see that?
- Mohu platit kartou? (MOH-hoo PLAH-teet KAR-toh) - Can I pay by card?
- To je příliš drahé. (toh yeh PREE-leesh DRAH-heh) - That's too expensive.
- Můžeme o tom jednat? (MOO-zheh-meh oh tom YED-nat) - Can we negotiate about it?

Practice these phrases before your trip, and don't hesitate to use them during your stay in Český Krumlov to show appreciation for the local culture and language.

With these resources at your disposal, you're well-equipped to make the most of your time in Český

Krumlov and ensure a smooth and memorable travel experience. Happy exploring!

Printed in Great Britain
by Amazon